What Others Are Saying about *We Thank Thee, O God, for a Prophet*

Chris Esseltine has produced a well-written piece that is both engaging and easy to follow. This work provides a well-organized and solid overview of this most important principles and, I believe, fulfills its goal to help members of the Church appreciate the living prophet and the role he plays in God's kingdom and the role he should play in our lives.

—Richard D. Draper
Associate Dean of Religious Education, Brigham Young University

It might be asked why we need a book on sustaining the prophet when members of the Church already raise their hands at every general conference. However, Mr. Esseltine's book details the specific way we are to do this, as revealed by the Lord to His servants, and he answers questions that many are reluctant to ask. I heartily recommend this book.

—Ronald M. Mann
former Special Assistant to President Ronald Reagan

WE THANK THEE, O GOD, FOR A PROPHET

WE THANK THEE, O GOD, FOR A PROPHET

A Guide to Sustaining the Living Prophet in the Latter Days

Christopher Esseltine

CFI
Springville, Utah

ISBN 13: 978-1-55517-952-2
ISBN 10: 1-55517-952-2

Published by CFI, an imprint of Cedar Fort, Inc., 925 N. Main, Springville, UT, 84663
Distributed by Cedar Fort, Inc. www.cedarfort.com

Cover design by Nicole Williams
Cover design © 2006 by Lyle Mortimer
Printed in the United States of America

10 9 8 7 6 5 4 3 2 1

Printed on acid-free paper

Dedication

To Joshua, the man who taught me what it means
to sustain the living prophet.

Table of Contents

Foreword

I developed the idea for this book a few years ago after hearing several differing views on the prophet's role and on our obligation as Saints to sustain him. I therefore wrote *We Thank Thee, O God, for a Prophet* for anyone who has a desire to more fully understand our relationship to the Lord's living oracle and what we need to do to stay in harmony with him. It introduces the reader to the most basic principles, and it systematically develops vital themes and doctrines to give a rich and in-depth perspective based on canonized scripture and the words of the living prophets of this dispensation.

This work not only offers a compendium of sources on this subject for teachers and students alike, but it also provides detailed and insightful responses to arguments posed by those who put little faith in the office of the living prophet. And while well-read Latter-day Saints may find a few sections to be simple review, I encourage them to keep reading—they'll be surprised at what they discover.

Acknowledgments

I express gratitude to my wife Adelia for spending countless hours evaluating and editing this work, and to Michael Morris for his interest in it.

CHAPTER ONE

The Importance of Prophets

A few months before I left on my mission, I was asked by a nonmember family I was close to what made my Church different from others they knew about. I was never intimidated by being put on the spot or being asked to discuss my religious beliefs; on the contrary, I looked forward to it. But this instance was tricky. I knew this family was not terribly religious, and they were sensitive about being preached to by anyone. My answer had to be brief, and it had to be unassuming so as not to seem what some people refer to as "holier than thou." Nevertheless, I wanted to do the question justice and leave a lasting impression on these people about how special and distinctive The Church of Jesus Christ of Latter-day Saints really is.

As I thought about the many things I could discuss—the platitudes, the clichés, the Sunday School answers—I started thinking about the Articles of Faith. Then the sixth Article of Faith came to me: "We believe in the same organization that existed in the Primitive Church, namely, apostles, prophets, pastors, teachers, evangelists, and so forth."

We have a prophet, called of God, with authority to minister in holy things on earth and to speak and act in the name of God! I began my response to this family by briefly recounting the Lord's dealings with His children on earth and showed that in every instance He raised up a prophet to organize the people and establish His will among them. I then posed the old missionary question: "If God loved His people enough to give them prophets in Old Testament times and loved them enough to give them prophets in New Testament times, doesn't it make sense that He still loves us enough to give us prophets in our day?"

The question, I know, is a little over simplified and perhaps a bit cheesy, but it captures the essence of the restored gospel. And although the mother of this family made a comment to her daughter the next day about me giving a sermon, I could tell the answer had a profound impact on the members of that family. I begin with this story to show the indispensable role prophets play in the plan of our Heavenly Father.

Although every member of the Church is at least somewhat familiar with prophets both ancient and modern, there is much yet to understand. The Lord has given us marvelous insights into His representatives and wants us to take advantage of this knowledge. By studying these insights, gaining a firm testimony of them, and implementing them in our personal lives, we can qualify for the choicest blessings that heaven can bestow.

The Purpose and Role of Prophets

The Fall of Adam

The introduction of prophets on earth began with the Fall of Adam. The true purpose and benefit of prophets can only be understood in this context. Insight into life prior to the Fall, the condition of the world after the Fall, and overcoming the effects of the Fall is essential to a proper knowledge of the role of the living prophet and the need to sustain him.

Before the Fall, Adam and Eve were in a state of innocence in which they experienced many things we cannot now enjoy. They lived in the presence of God, they walked and talked with Him as He pleased, and they were continually filled with at least a portion of celestial glory. They did not need to work to eat or survive because food grew plentifully. In fact, no weeds grew and plants had no prickers, needles, or poisonous properties. Adam and Eve needed no clothing because the earth's climate was perfectly suited to their bodies—they never got hot or cold. They were never in danger because everything lived in peace upon the earth—lions didn't bite, sharks didn't attack swimmers, and bees didn't sting.

After Eve and Adam voluntarily partook of the forbidden fruit, however, things changed dramatically. First, they both realized they had been living in a state of innocence in which they never really appreciated anything because they knew no differently. Eating the fruit gave them knowledge of the difference between good and evil. Eating the fruit also changed their bodies. They became mortal and subject not only to death but also to weakness, pain, sickness, hunger, and fatigue. This allowed them to have children and start the process by which the hosts of heaven could obtain bodies. However, Eve (and all women thereafter) had to endure the physical and emotional hardships associated with childbirth.

The Fall affected much more than just Adam and Eve. The whole earth fell. All the animals became mortal and had to compete with one another to survive. This established the food chain in which beasts that were formerly friendly began eating one another. The trees and plants that yielded a limitless supply of food were restricted by their own mortality and developed natural defenses against predators and the elements. The climate also changed dramatically. To protect themselves against the elements and against the rough and tumble of the world, Adam and Eve were forced to wear the skins of animals. In short, the Fall transformed the earth from a paradisiacal state into the lone and dreary world.

Speaking of the effects of the Fall, the Lord told Adam: "Cursed shall be the ground for thy sake; in sorrow shalt thou eat of it all the days of thy life. Thorns also, and thistles shall it bring forth to thee, and thou shalt eat the herb of the field. By the sweat of thy face shalt thou eat bread, until thou shalt return unto the ground—for thou shalt surely die" (Moses 4:23–25).

The most profound effect of the Fall by far was that the earth and all things on it—including Adam and Eve and their future children—were cast out of the presence of God. They could no longer speak with Him the same way, they weren't able to look upon Him with their natural eyes, and their limited mental abilities were not sufficient to comprehend heavenly things the way they could before. Being cast out of God's presence meant more than simply not being with Him anymore. It meant a drastic withdrawal of the spirit. This spirit, or what the scriptures also call glory, is the life by which God quickens all things and by which He has power (D&C 33:16).

It was this glory that protected the earth from mortality, suffering, and chaos prior to the Fall of Adam. It enabled Adam and Eve to be as familiar with heavenly things every second of the day as Joseph Smith was in the Sacred Grove for only a short while. It gave them revelatory abilities of life that transcended the five measly senses humans now have at their disposal.[1] Once that glory was taken away, Adam and Eve—and the entire earth—were left spiritually damaged. It was as if one of us was suddenly made deaf and blind and dropped off in the middle of the desert far from any family or friends to help us. In a very real sense, Adam and Eve experienced a similar condition.

Section 29 of the Doctrine and Covenants refers to this removal from God's presence and the withdrawal of His glory as "spiritual death." The Lord revealed: "Wherefore, I, the Lord God, caused that he [Adam] should be cast out from the Garden of Eden, from my presence, because of his transgression, wherein he became spiritually dead" (D&C 29:41).

President Joseph F. Smith discussed the concept of spiritual death further, speaking about "another death, which is a more terrible death than that of the body." He stated that when "Adam, our first parent, partook of the forbidden fruit, transgressed the law of God, and became subject unto Satan, he was banished from the presence of God, and was thrust out into . . . spiritual darkness. This was the first death. Yet living, he was dead—dead to God, dead to light and truth, dead spiritually, cast out from the presence of God; communication between the Father and the Son was cut off. He was absolutely thrust out from the presence of God as was Satan and the hosts that followed him. That was spiritual death."[2]

Adam's Fall brought physical and spiritual death into the world, and by so doing, he began the process by which all of Heavenly Father's children could come to earth, obtain a body, be proved in a mortal probation, and decide for themselves through agency where they wanted to dwell for eternity. As a part of this process, all of these children (including you and me) forget their heavenly abode when they come to earth and forget their premortal relationship with their Heavenly Father. Orson Pratt explained this when he taught that the Fall "has let down a veil between us and our Father and God. . . . It prevents us, while in this state of mortality, from beholding his presence, unless we rend the veil by our faith and obedience and, like the brother of Jared, are permitted to come back into his presence. . . . We are now laboring under the imperfections of the fall, and because of that fall a veil shuts us from his presence."[3]

The Fall was Part of the Plan

Before anyone curses Adam or Eve for partaking of the forbidden fruit and bringing death into the world, it should be made clear that the Fall was an indispensable part of our Heavenly Father's plan. In order to truly be proved and work out a salvation before the Lord, every person in the spirit world (except those who were cast out with Lucifer for rebellion) needed to come to earth, receive a body, experience the challenges of a mortal probation, and finally pass through death.

In one of his last great discourses, father Lehi taught his posterity about the need for the Fall. He explained:

> And to bring about his eternal purposes in the end of man, after he [God] had created our first parents, and . . . all things which are created, it must needs be that there was an opposition; even the forbidden fruit. . . .
>
> And now, behold, if Adam had not transgressed he would not have fallen, but he would have remained in the garden of Eden. And all things which were created must have remained in the same state in which they were after they were created; and they must have remained forever, and had no end.
>
> And they would have had no children; wherefore they would have remained in a state of innocence, having no joy, for they knew no misery; doing no good, for they knew no sin.
>
> But behold, all things have been done in the wisdom of him who knoweth all things.
>
> Adam fell that men might be; and men are, that they might have joy. And the Messiah cometh in the fulness of time, that he may redeem the children of men from the fall." (2 Nephi 2:15, 22–26)

Adam, the First Prophet

After Adam and Eve were cast out of the presence of God, their most important and pressing goal was to return to what they had—to get back into the presence of a loving Heavenly Father in this mortal life and enjoy the infusion of life-giving celestial glory. Because Adam and Eve had already experienced celestial glory in God's presence, their only real desire was to return to it and bring their posterity with them. They knew how good it was and how painful life was without it, and they were willing to do anything to reclaim it. They pled with the Lord for guidance on how to accomplish this, and in His own time, the Lord answered their prayers.

The scriptures record that "Adam and Eve, his wife, called upon the name of the Lord, and they heard the voice of the Lord from the way toward the Garden of Eden, speaking unto them, and they saw him not; for they were shut out from his presence. And he gave unto them commandments, that they should worship the Lord their God, and should offer the firstlings of their flocks, for an offering unto the Lord. And Adam was obedient unto the commandments of the Lord" (Moses 5:4–5).

As Adam and Eve were obedient to the Lord's commandments (even when they admitted they did not know what the purpose was), an angel appeared and declared more of the gospel to them. The angel explained that a Savior had been appointed to come to redeem mankind and the whole earth from the effects of the Fall. Because of the great infusion of truth and light given through this heavenly minister, "The Holy Ghost fell upon Adam, which beareth record of the Father and the Son, saying: I am the Only Begotten of the Father from the beginning, henceforth and forever, that as thou hast fallen thou mayest be redeemed, and all mankind, even as many as will" (Moses 5:9).

After the Holy Ghost fell upon Adam, he was transformed and filled with a portion of glory to such an extent that he "blessed God and was filled, and began to prophesy concerning all the families of the earth, saying: Blessed be the name of God, for because of my transgression my eyes are opened, and in this life I shall have joy, and again in the flesh I shall see God. And Eve, his wife, heard all these things and was glad, saying: Were it not for our transgression we never should have had seed, and never should have known good and evil, and the joy of our redemption, and the eternal life which God giveth unto all the obedient" (Moses 5:10–11).

After Adam and Eve were filled with knowledge, truth, light, and glory, they then "made all things known unto their sons and their daughters" (Moses 5:12).

The most important thing to Adam and Eve after they had received their own witness of the Spirit and had been endowed with glory was to share this tremendous gift with the rest of mankind. They wanted their children to experience the same glory and joy they did, and they wanted all their posterity to return back to the presence of the Lord–especially in this life. At this point, Adam became the first prophet of the human race.[4]

The Prophet Joseph Smith taught that "the Priesthood was first given to Adam: he obtained the First Presidency, and held the keys of it from generation to generation" and he had "dominion given him over every creature."[5] Adam was the "first and father of all, not only by progeny, but the first to hold the spiritual blessings, to whom was made known the plan of ordinances for the salvation of his posterity unto the end, and to whom Christ was first revealed, and through whom Christ has been revealed from heaven."[6]

Some of Adam's posterity chose to follow the Lord and many others did not, but Adam remained the Lord's living prophet over the whole earth and guided many into God's presence to enjoy His glory, even though they remained for several years in their mortal probation upon the earth. Shortly before his death, father Adam gathered his posterity to him and, once again, taught them how to return to God's presence. Commenting by way of personal revelation about this event, the Prophet explained, "I saw Adam in the valley of Adam-ondi-Ahman. He called together his children and blessed them with a patriarchal blessing. The Lord appeared in their midst, and he (Adam) blessed them all, and foretold what should befall them to the latest generation. This is why Adam blessed his posterity; he wanted to bring them into the presence of God."[7]

Succession of Prophets

Because Adam was mortal, the Lord prepared a way for all mankind in every age to continue to have access to the light, truth, knowledge, and glory that Adam offered them. After Adam's death, other prophets continued to be raised up, all working to teach the children of men how to return to the glory that Adam and Eve enjoyed in the garden. Next in line to Adam was his son Abel. But because Abel was murdered by his brother Cain, Seth was appointed in his place. After Seth came Enos, Cainan, Mahalaleel, Jared, and Enoch.

Each of these had one main objective: to bring God's children into His presence, to endow them with the glory Adam and Eve enjoyed before the Fall. The scriptures seem to indicate that Enoch was the first prophet since Adam to successfully apply the gospel program to such an extent that he and his people were able to enjoy the glory of God's presence while on the earth.

The Bible reveals little about the prophet Enoch, but the Pearl of Great Price provides valuable insight into this remarkable man and his people. The book of Moses reveals that Enoch "saw the Lord; and he stood before my face, and he talked with me, even as a man talketh one with another, face to face" (Moses 7:4). The Lord commanded him to organize the righteous who would follow and build a holy city. The record then states:

> So great was the faith of Enoch that he led the people of God, and their enemies came to battle against them; and he spake the word of the Lord, and the earth trembled, and the mountains fled, even according to his command . . . and all nations feared greatly, so powerful was the word of Enoch. . . . The fear of the Lord was upon all nations, so great was the *glory* of the Lord, which was upon his people." (Moses 7: 13, 17; emphasis added)

The glory spoken of in this passage that struck fear into the hearts of the wicked nations was the same glory that spiritually renewed and enlivened the people of Enoch. It transformed them, and they, through Christ, overcame many of the effects of the Fall.

Had the wicked children of the world repented and followed Enoch, the whole earth could have become like the City of Enoch—endowed with glory, able to abide the presence of the Lord, and transformed to an Eden-like state with access to many of the life-giving powers Adam and Eve enjoyed. But because Enoch's people reached this state of glory and the rest of the world continued to grow more wicked, the record reveals that "Zion have I blessed, but the residue of the people have I cursed" (Moses 7:20).

Enoch and his people were taken from the wicked earth, and the Lord made Noah the prophet to the world. And after God destroyed all but Noah's family in the great flood, Noah immediately began teaching his posterity, just as Adam had done, about the gospel and the path to return to God's presence. In fact, whenever the Lord has had a people who have not completely rejected Him, He has blessed them with living prophets to teach, guide, and endow the people with truth, light, and glory.

Although the majority of the newly populated earth once again began to embrace wickedness only a few years after the flood, many of Noah's posterity followed the prophets God raised up. From Melchizedek to Abraham, Isaac, and Jacob, the tradition of prophets continued, as did their mission to lead mankind back to God's presence both in this life and in the next.

And even though some of the teachings of the various prophets throughout history may seem to deal more with living a good life in the fallen world rather than preparing us to return to the Garden of Eden, the gospel program has always focused on returning to God's presence here and now, just as Enoch's people did.

For example, when Israel suffered under the yoke of Egyptian bondage, Moses was appointed and called to lead them to the promised land. However, his primary purpose was not simply to free them from Pharaoh's tyranny; it was to free them from the effects of the Fall. The Prophet Joseph Smith taught that the great Levite prophet "sought to bring the children of Israel into the presence of God, through the power of the priesthood, but he could not. In the first ages of the world they tried to establish the same thing; and there were [prophets] raised up who tried to restore these very glories, but did not obtain them; but they prophesied of a day when this glory would be revealed. Paul spoke of the dispensation of the fullness of times, when God would gather together all things in one."[8]

Moses was not just trying to establish ten commandments to maintain order in society, nor simply to give Israel a restored Church. He offered them a chance to build the same type of society that Enoch's people had built. Moses had received glory sufficient to enjoy God's presence, but Israel proved too stubborn to accept what the Lord had offered so many times before. They "hardened their hearts and could not endure his presence" (D&C 84:24). For centuries after Moses, the Lord sent prophets to proclaim the word of the Lord and to gather the righteous to come into His presence. But again, only a few dedicated souls were ever able to take advantage of the gospel program.

However, the Prophet Joseph Smith revealed in the above passage that all the prophets knew the chance to lead God's covenant people back to Him would be given once again in the last dispensation—our dispensation. The Prophet Joseph himself was raised up to accomplish this task. The ultimate end of all he worked for was to endow the Saints with glory, build Zion, and bring Israel back into God's presence. Joseph revealed to the Saints that Christ "grants this privilege of seeing and knowing for themselves; that through the power and manifestations of the Spirit, while in the flesh, they may be able to bear his presence in the world of glory" (D&C 76:117–18). Joseph stated elsewhere, "Could we all come together with one heart and one mind in perfect faith the veil might as well be rent today as next week, or any other time, and if we will but cleanse ourselves and covenant before God, to serve Him, it is our privilege to have an assurance that God will protect us at all times."[9]

Other revelations emphasize the promise that fallen man can come into God's presence in this life. For example, the Lord taught that the temple is such a vital and sacred part of the gospel program because "my glory shall be there, and my presence shall be there. . . . For I will come into it, and all the pure in heart that shall come into it shall see God" (D&C 94:8; 97:16). He also taught that one of the powers of the Melchizedek Priesthood is to have "the privilege of receiving the mysteries of the kingdom of heaven, to have the heavens opened unto them, to commune with the general assembly and church of the Firstborn, and to enjoy the communion and presence of God the Father, and Jesus the mediator of the new covenant" (D&C 107:19).

Since the Prophet Joseph Smith was martyred and sealed his testimony with his blood, the Lord has continued to bless His Saints with prophets to lead, guide, direct, and prepare His people to return to His presence.

Prophets—Indispensable to God's Plan

After reading the account of the Fall, some might ask, "Why couldn't God just speak to the righteous who were willing to listen and reveal to them individually by the Spirit how to return? Do we really need prophets?" These are fair questions. The quickest answer (albeit somewhat unsatisfying) is, "Yes, we do need prophets." But there is the question of why. The first and most obvious answer is that God wants it that way. The scriptures make it extremely clear that the plan of our Heavenly Father requires prophets. For example, Amos taught, "Surely the Lord God will do *nothing,* but he revealeth his secret unto his servants the prophets" (Amos 3:7; emphasis added).

Speaking of Israel, the Lord declared to Moses, "I will raise them up a Prophet from among their brethren . . . and will put my words in his mouth; and he shall speak unto them all that I shall command him" (Deuteronomy 18:18).

The role of prophets is again confirmed as 2 Kings reveals: "Yet the Lord testified against Israel, and against Judah, by all the prophets, and by all the seers, saying, Turn ye from your evil ways, and keep my commandments and my statutes, according to all the law which I commanded your fathers, and which I sent to you by my servants the prophets" (2 Kings 17:13).

There are those (mainly of other faiths) who have read these scriptures and believe that, because they are found in the Old Testament, they refer exclusively to the period of time preceding the birth, ministry, atonement, and resurrection of Christ. They argue that God sent prophets into the world just until Jesus came to fulfill the law. After that, they reason, Christ gave mankind everything it needed to be saved—which can be found in the New Testament—and, therefore, prophets are no longer needed. However, the New Testament contains many references to the essential and continuing role of prophets. For example, describing the way the Lord himself organized His Church, Paul explained, "And he gave some, apostles; and some, *prophets*; and some, evangelists; and some, pastors and teachers; for the perfecting of the saints, for the work of the ministry, for the edifying of the body of Christ" (Ephesians 4:11–12; emphasis added).

Paul also made it clear that the gospel "is now revealed unto his holy apostles and prophets by the Spirit" (Ephesians 3:5).

In our modern dispensation, when the gospel program has been restored, the Lord revealed that the "laws of the kingdom . . . are given by the prophets of God" (D&C 58:18).

What Is a Prophet?

The scriptures witness that prophets are key to the gospel plan and the operation of the Church, but we must understand exactly what a prophet is and what it means to be one. In the broadest sense of the word, the scriptures teach that anyone who has a testimony of Jesus is a prophet. John the Revelator taught that "the testimony of Jesus is the spirit of prophecy" (Revelation 19:10). The Prophet Joseph Smith reiterated this when he declared, "No man is a minister of Jesus Christ without being a prophet."[10] For "the testimony of Jesus is the spirit of prophecy."[11]

In more conservative terms, a prophet is someone who has been called by God and set apart for several specific purposes. First, a prophet acts as the Lord's spokesman to His people and to the world (D&C 100:9). He stands in place of the Lord on earth to act as His personal authorized representative (D&C 84:36). A prophet testifies of Christ in all things (D&C 20:26) and is a lawgiver to the people (D&C 58:18). A prophet writes and interprets scripture (D&C 35:20; 68:4) and holds the keys to unlock knowledge and power that is sealed (D&C 35:18). Prophets are teachers who instruct and guide mankind in the ways of Godliness; Moses referred to them as "preachers of righteousness" who "spake and prophesied, and called upon all men, everywhere, to repent" (Moses 6:23). Indeed, prophets do call men to repentance when necessary (D&C 6:9). And as the name might indicate, a prophet also prophesies and declares the future, or possible future, to mortal man (1 Nephi 22:2).

In its greatest expression and meaning, the term prophet refers to the one man who stands at the head of the kingdom on earth to lead and direct the people on behalf of the Lord (D&C 107:91–92). He is the person in whom all the authority, rights, keys, and privileges pertaining to the kingdom on earth are vested. Although all members of the Church who have a testimony of Jesus could be considered prophets, and although apostles are considered "Prophets, Seers, Revelators, and special witnesses to all the nations of the earth,"[12] there is only one man at a time on earth who is considered by the Lord and by the Church as *the* prophet.

The Living Prophet

Let us return to that all-important question: "What makes The Church of Jesus Christ of Latter-day Saints different from all other churches?" The answer is revealed in the first section of the Doctrine and Covenants. The Lord discusses His church, telling the Saints, "And also those to whom these commandments were given, might have power to lay the foundation of this church, and to bring it forth out of obscurity and out of darkness, the *only* true and *living* church upon the face of the whole earth" (D&C 1:30; emphasis added).

The Lord refers to His Church as the only *living* Church on the earth. Arguably then, the most dramatic difference between Christ's restored Church and all others is not the doctrine, or the structural organization, or even the name, but rather the fact that it is a *living* Church.

The term "living" is meaningful in at least three ways. First, the Church is the only organization on earth authorized by the Lord to perform valid and divinely sanctioned ordinances that lead to salvation. While other churches claim their authority from various sources, the authority to minister in the name of God was taken from the earth during the Apostasy. Simply reading about this Church or studying the original gospel pattern from the pages of the Bible bestows no authority to perform ordinances or declare revelation on behalf of the Lord.

By contrast, The Church of Jesus Christ of Latter-day Saints is the *restored* Church authorized to perform living, divinely recognized ordinances. President Joseph F. Smith taught that this authority is so essential because "nearly everything depends upon it. No ordinance can be performed to the acceptance of God without divine authority. No matter how fervently men may believe or pray, unless they are endowed with divine authority they can only act in their own name, and not legally nor acceptably in the name of Jesus Christ, in whose name all things must be done." He continued by asserting: "Some suppose this authority may be derived from the Bible, but nothing could be more absurd. The Bible is but a book containing the writings of inspired men . . . but this does not give me authority to teach men in the name of the Lord, nor to officiate in the sacred ordinances of the gospel."[13]

The second way the Church is living is that because it is Christ's authorized church, it has the right to the infusion of the life, light, truth, power, and glory that leads people to Christ. President Gordon B. Hinckley affirmed that "wherever the Church is organized its power is felt."[14] Brigham Young taught that The Church of Jesus Christ of Latter-day Saints is so attractive to the pure in heart because "it is a system of power; it is because there are gifts connected with it. . . . It is because there are in this Church prophets and apostles, the gifts of revelation, of healing, and discerning of spirits, and all the other gifts, that were ever enjoyed by the ancient people of God." President Young continued, explaining that these gifts "make the Church of Jesus Christ a power in the earth," and make "the teachings and doctrines of this Church so attractive to all the inhabitants of the earth who believe truthfully and sincerely the doctrines contained in the Old and New Testaments. It supplies the want that is felt by every honest heart, a yearning after the knowledge of God . . . and a yearning that dispels all darkness and disbelief."[15]

When the Prophet Joseph Smith and other leading brethren traveled to Washington D.C. to petition the government for redress, President Martin Van Buren asked how the Mormons differed from other religions. The Prophet took the opportunity to expound on how the Church was a living body. The account of his response states that in his interview with the President, he was asked "wherein we differed in our religion from the other religions of the day. Brother Joseph said we differed in mode of baptism, and the gift of the Holy Ghost by the laying on of hands. We considered that all other considerations were contained in [the answer] *the gift of the Holy Ghost.*"[16] According to Joseph then, the Spirit makes this a living Church.

The third way in which the Church is living is that it is the only one that receives continual, living revelation and guidance directly from Jesus

Christ. In ancient times, the Church relied upon continuing revelation for its very life. When Christ left the Church in the hands of the Apostles and returned to the Father, He laid the keys of the kingdom on Peter, making him chief apostle, prophet, and president of the Church. The Savior explained to His prophet, "Thou are Peter, and upon this rock I will build my church; and the gates of hell shall not prevail against it" (Matthew 16:18).

The Savior reiterated the same sentiment in this dispensation when He said, "And upon this rock I will build my church; yea, upon this rock ye are built, and if ye continue, the gates of hell shall not prevail against you" (D&C 33:13). The Prophet Joseph Smith explained these declarations, stating, "Jesus in His teaching says, 'Upon this rock I will build my Church, and the gates of hell shall not prevail against it.' What rock? Revelation."[17] Continuing revelation is therefore absolutely necessary to a living church.

If a church must have continuing revelation in order for it to be considered living, it must be led by a prophet who receives continuing revelation from Christ Himself. There have been many prophets on the earth since Adam, but a prophet who is alive and present and continually directing the kingdom is more significant than past prophets whose words speak to the Saints from the pages of scripture. He must be a living, breathing man who continues to receive revelation from the Lord at any given moment.

Because this prophet is alive and stands at the head of the Church, he differs from all other prophets who have come before him. First, he is alive in our day; second, he receives living, continuing, current revelation from the Lord. For these two reasons, he is appropriately referred to as the "living prophet," the prophet who has the right to speak on behalf of the Lord at a given time. The living prophet is the one man who is called as the chief presiding authority at the most current time—either now or twenty years from now.

Just before the great flood, Noah was the living prophet, even though men like Adam and Enoch preceded him. When Israel wandered the desert for forty years, Moses was the living prophet, even though they observed the teachings of Abraham, Isaac, and Jacob. And although the Jewish leaders of the first century A.D. held fast to the law of Moses, Peter was the living prophet they were supposed to follow.

Need for a Living Prophet

Let us return to the question, "Why can't God just speak to individuals and teach them how to get back to His presence. Why do we need prophets?" As indicated earlier in this chapter, the most important reason is because God wants it that way. But the Lord has revealed some specific reasons as well. First, we are all individuals and are, therefore, distinct, diverse, and unique. Because of this, we are all at different stages in our spiritual and emotional development. Not everyone is equally righteous, as prepared to sacrifice as much as another, or as educated about the doctrines of the Church. Some people have trouble forgiving, some are challenged by lusts of the flesh, and others set their hearts too much on the things of this world. Whatever the issues, common sense tells us that not everyone stands at the same place spiritually.

It is, therefore, reasonable to assume that not everyone has the same relationship with the Lord. Some are closer to Him because they have given themselves to Him in love and obedience with a much greater commitment than others. They have sought diligently to get closer to Him because He promised, "Draw near unto me and I will draw near unto you; seek me diligently and ye shall find me" (D&C 88:63).

Who would dispute that the Prophet Joseph Smith had a closer relationship with the Lord than most? Abraham also did because he sacrificed everything to find the God of his fathers. Many men and women, aside from prophets, have developed a close and very personal relationship with the Lord because they committed themselves to Him. But this does not mean that most of God's people throughout history have truly sought Him the way they needed to. And because of this, not everyone enjoys the same level of spiritual development.

With this in mind, it is much easier to understand that not everyone is prepared to communicate directly with the Lord and have Him personally reveal those things that will bring them back into His presence. Therefore, we need a living prophet who *has* developed a personal intimate relationship with the Lord to guide the rest of us who are still working to get there.

Another reason living prophets are essential is that God's kingdom is one of order. He Himself proclaimed, "Behold, mine house is a house of order, saith the Lord God, and not a house of confusion" (D&C 132:8).

To maintain this order, the Lord has appointed one man on earth to administer the affairs of His kingdom. This man (the living prophet and president of the Church) then appoints others by revelation because "all things must be done in order, and by common consent in the church, by the prayer of faith" (D&C 28:13).

It would not do, for example, to have every person exercising an equal degree of control over the Church. Think of the result of millions of people receiving millions of different revelations about the same issue. At least some of them, if not most, would contradict each other. How would questions get resolved? Could a simple majority consensus settle the matter? Of course not; the kingdom of God is not a democracy. To lead by a majority vote would create confusion, contention, and ultimately chaos. This does not mean that individuals have no agency in the Church—quite the contrary. But like all stable, just, wise, and prosperous systems, leadership vested in a spokesman creates order.

This is how the priesthood is organized. The Father delegates power and authority to the Son, who in turn calls and ordains prophets. These men ordain others to priesthood offices by inspiration in an order of hierarchical succession. Each person who is called under the direction of the living prophet then has the right and responsibility to preside over a particular stewardship. Just as it would not do to have four fathers in one household each receiving revelation for the family or to have ten bishops presiding over a ward, chaos would ensue if more than one person held the authority to preside over the Church.

A third reason for a living prophet is unity. Some might argue that if all Church members could receive revelation for themselves, everyone would agree and get along because the same Spirit would guide them all, eliminating confusion and chaos. The first problem with this argument is that history has proven it false. For example, how well did Israel do when Moses left to commune with Jehovah on Mount Sinai? The book of Acts reveals that even the early Apostles had "no small dissension and disputation with them" (Acts 15:2) concerning a particular point of doctrine. Later, the missionary companionship of Paul and Barnabas had such a falling out that the record states, "The contention was so sharp between them, that they departed asunder one from another" (Acts 15:39). The history of the early days of the restoration is filled with instances of disharmony, disunity, and dysfunction. The Lord revealed time and again the many blessings that were denied the Saints because of their failure to be obedient to the Prophet and united under him (see D&C 67:10; 84:55–57; 105:2–5).

Any group of Saints that could be united enough to all agree perfectly on every truth, doctrine, or pearl of knowledge would probably already be in God's presence enjoying celestial glory. They would be like the City of Enoch who were called "Zion, because they were of one heart and one mind, and dwelt in righteousness; and there was no poor among them" (Moses 7:18). But the house of Israel has a disposition for the kind of pride, greed, covetousness, and unrighteousness that prevents a people from producing the unity necessary to live in God's presence.

Remember, the purpose of prophets is to reveal to God's children how to return to His presence and enjoy celestial glory. Prophets are called because the people don't know these things firsthand without being shown them. Adam and Eve's offspring never lived in the Garden of Eden; Enoch's people did not speak with the Lord face to face until Enoch showed them how; Israel never experienced the burning bush on Mount Sinai; you and I never experienced the First Vision. The fact that we aren't now in God's presence should indicate that perhaps we don't know all we need to. If all God's children were spiritually mature enough to do it for themselves, we would have many more accounts of cities like Enoch's being taken up to heaven, or perhaps the earth would already be restored to a state like the Garden of Eden.

Knowing what prophets are, what a living prophet is, what his responsibilities are, and how indispensable he is to the gospel plan is the first step to sustaining a prophet. However, some differing views and opinions exist about exactly how to do this. We as Latter-day Saints need to know what we are required to do and not do, what to believe and not believe.

Thankfully, the Lord has revealed certain keys to understanding how to sustain His living prophet. They are contained in the standard works and the teachings of other prophets. The next seven chapters of this book will outline and discuss the principles that every Latter-day Saint needs to understand and be committed to in order to properly sustain the living prophet and reap the blessings the Lord has promised to those who heed His servants.

Notes

1. See Moses 1. After being endowed with just a portion of God's Spirit, Moses was transfigured and able to endure the presence of God, to behold and comprehend every person, intelligence, and particle of the earth at once. This is the glory that Adam and Eve enjoyed in the garden. Compared to this spiritual ability, their

senses after the Fall can appropriately be considered measly.

2. Joseph F. Smith, *Gospel Doctrine: Selections from the Sermons and Writings of Joseph F. Smith* (Salt Lake City: Deseret News, 1919), 432.
3. John A. Widtsoe, in *Journal of Discourses,* 26 vols. (London: Latter-day Saints' Book Depot, 1854–86), 16:364.
4. This refers to the earth, not to the premortal spirit world or to other mortal worlds apart from this planet.
5. Joseph Smith, *Teachings of the Prophet Joseph Smith,* sel. Joseph Fielding Smith (Salt Lake City: Deseret Book, 1976), 157.
6. Ibid., 167.
7. Ibid., 158–59.
8. Ibid., 159.
9. Ibid., 9.
10. Ibid., 160.
11. Ibid., 119.
12. Ibid., 109.
13. Joseph F. Smith, in *Journal of Discourses,* 19:191.
14. Gordon B. Hinckley, "Testimony," *Ensign,* May 1998, 69.
15. Brigham Young, in *Journal of Discourses,* 19:109.
16. Joseph Smith, *History of The Church of Jesus Christ of Latter-day Saints,* ed. B. H. Roberts, 2d ed. rev., 7 vols. (Salt Lake City: The Church of Jesus Christ of Latter-day Saints, 1932–51), 4:42.
17. Smith, *Teachings,* 274.

CHAPTER TWO

Principle 1: Revelation and Commandments are Given through the Living Prophet

As discussed in chapter 1, continuing revelation is essential to the living Church of Jesus Christ of Latter-day Saints. Wilford Woodruff once expressed, "The Church of God could not live twenty-four hours without revelation."[1] Because prophets are a fundamental part of the gospel, it follows that continuing revelation to the Church comes through the living prophet. Consider the Lord's declaration in the Doctrine and Covenants on this matter. In section 21, He spoke of His living prophet: "Thou shalt give heed unto *all* his [the Prophet's] words and commandments which he shall give unto you as he receiveth them, walking in all holiness before me; for his word ye shall receive as if from mine own mouth" (D&C 21:4–5; emphasis added).

The Lord reiterated this passage in section 1, where He proclaimed, "Whether by mine own voice or by the voice of my servants, it is the same" (D&C 1:38).

Section 58 teaches that Church officers, such as bishops, are to judge Israel "according to the laws of the kingdom which are given by the prophets of God" (D&C 58:18).

Prophets, Seers, and Revelators

At every general, stake, and ward conference in the Church, each member has the special opportunity and privilege of affirming, upholding, and sustaining the living prophet and other Church leaders. One of the specific things members acknowledge is the calling of the living prophet, his counselors, and the Twelve Apostles as prophets, seers, and revelators. However, the exact meanings of the terms "prophet," "seer," and "revelator" and how they relate to Church leadership can often be unclear.

Each of these terms, although distinct in their exact meanings, are closely associated with one another and are related to the same objectives and purposes. The term prophet, in its most exclusive sense, has been defined in the previous chapter as someone who has been ordained and set apart to receive revelation for the Church as a whole.

A seer is exactly what the word denotes—one who sees. A person who is a seer is empowered to see things beyond mortal capacity. For example, a seer can see "things which are past, and also . . . things which are to come." Through seers "shall all things be revealed, or, rather, shall secret things be made manifest, and hidden things shall come to light" (Mosiah 8:17).

Those who have heavenly visions and dreams are seers, though they may not have the keys to bind others by what they receive for themselves. Those who can interpret these dreams because they have likewise viewed them by the Spirit are seers. The ancient patriarch Joseph, who was sold into Egypt, was one of these. He saw in vision the seven years of plenty and the seven years of famine and was able to interpret Pharaoh's dream accordingly. Seers also have the ability to "translate all records" (Mosiah 8:13) and read unknown languages. The Prophet Joseph Smith did this when he translated the book of Mormon, the book of Abraham, and the Book of Moses.[2] In short, anyone who has been given revelation by visual means is a seer. It is such a sacred gift, in fact, that "a seer is greater than a prophet . . . and a gift which is greater can no man have" (Mosiah 8:15–16).

Like a prophet, a seer needs no specific calling or designation to receive divine visual manifestations. But also like a prophet, a seer needs to be ordained and set apart as a seer to the Church in order for his revelations to be binding. Connected with the gift of being a seer is the use of sacred revelatory tools known as "seer stones." The most famous of these are the Urim and Thummim, through which the Prophet translated the Book of Mormon. However, only those ordained and authorized can use these instruments. For example, Ammon explained that the Urim and Thummim are also called "interpreters, and no man can look in them except he be commanded. . . And whosoever is commanded to look in them, the same is called a seer" (Mosiah 8:13).

Anyone may have the gift of being a seer, but only authorized persons have full right to use the instruments of seership and to reveal what they have seen to the Church as a whole.

The term revelator also means exactly what the word denotes: one who reveals. To be a revelator requires two things: first, receiving revelation from God, and second, revealing it to someone. Revelation comes in many forms, including heavenly visitations, dreams, visions, voices, insights, and inspiration. And like the designation of prophet and seer, only those specially called and set apart have the right to act as revelators to the entire Church.

Some further clarification needs to be made of each of these terms and their relationship to one another. A prophet is a revelator because he both receives revelation and gives it to others. For example, a true testimony of Christ must be revealed from the heavens. Bearing that testimony—whether a ward member in sacrament meeting or the president of the Church in an official proclamation—is an act of revealing to others. A seer can also be considered a revelator because he receives divine visual revelation and then reveals it in some way.

However, a prophet is not necessarily a seer. Although he may be, it is possible to have a testimony of Christ and even have the right to bear that testimony to the world without seeing the future in vision, translating through seer stones, or receiving other visual revelation. For the same reason, a revelator is not necessarily a seer, but may be.

The abilities and blessings of prophets, seers, and revelators are available to everyone, or at least to everyone the Lord chooses to bless with them. They are not exclusive to the president of the Church. For example, the Twelve Apostles are ordained and sustained prophets, seers, and revelators to the Church (under the direction of the First Presidency); a Stake President may reveal the will of the Lord to members of his stake, parents may receive and reveal revelation on behalf of their families.

These blessings are also not restricted by age or gender. The Prophet

Joseph Smith taught that anyone who has a "testimony of Jesus" possesses "the spirit of prophecy."[3] The Lord testified that the gospel was established so that "*every man* [person] might speak in the name of God the Lord, even the Savior of the world" (D&C 1:20; emphasis added). Joel prophesied: "And it shall come to pass afterward, that I will pour out my spirit upon all flesh; and your sons and your daughters shall prophesy, your old men shall dream dreams, your young men shall see visions: and also upon the servants and upon the handmaids in those days will I pour out my spirit" (Joel 2:28–29; see also Acts 2:17–19).

Every Latter-day Saint may qualify to receive the spirit of prophecy and other gifts of the Spirit, but the true prophets, seers, and revelators for the Church are found in the First Presidency and the Quorum of the Twelve Apostles. These are the men who have been ordained to receive and use these blessings on behalf of the whole Church.

Two Channels of Revelation

There are two channels of revelation in the Church—that is, two main ways by which revelation is given to men on earth. The first comes through the Holy Ghost and is given directly to the hearts and minds of worthy individuals. This is the most common kind of revelation. Every person who has been baptized and received the gift of the Holy Ghost by one holding authority has the right to revelation through the Holy Ghost.

The scriptures teach that the Holy Ghost is the Spirit of God and the "Spirit is truth" (1 John 5:6), which "witnesses of the Father and the Son" (2 Nephi 31:18). The Holy Ghost teaches us "all things" (John 14:26) and helps us discern truth from error. The Holy Ghost also prompts us with insight and inspiration and moves us to speak (D&C 68:4), showing us all things we should do (2 Nephi 32:5). He is referred to as the "Comforter" (John 14:26) and acts as a constant companion to the righteous (D&C 121:46). The Holy Ghost enlivens and quickens us with life (Moses 6:65) and cleanses us of our sins (2 Nephi 31:17). The Holy Ghost is the means by which mankind receives spiritual gifts and through which revelation comes. The Prophet Joseph Smith taught, "No man can receive the Holy Ghost without receiving revelations. The Holy Ghost is a revelator."[4]

Personal revelation through the Holy Ghost is given for various reasons. It most often comes in direct answer to prayer. Sometimes special needs are fulfilled, sometimes doctrinal principles are taught, and sometimes men and women receive testimony and confirmation about a gospel truth. The Holy Ghost can comfort us in times of despair, change our hearts and minds, turn us from sin, warn us in times of danger, or give us insight about others who could use our help.

Personal revelation through the Holy Ghost also comes in various ways. This does not mean the Holy Ghost is inconsistent. It is revealed to everyone in *generally* the same way. The Apostle Paul taught, "But the fruit of the Spirit is love, joy, peace, longsuffering, gentleness, goodness, faith, meekness, temperance" (Galatians 5:22–23).

Regardless of how the Spirit manifests itself to an individual, it always fosters goodness. But even though this is how the Holy Ghost operates in a general sense, every member of the Church is an individual, and, therefore, revelatory experiences are given to different people in different ways at different times.

For example, sometimes revelation comes to people's minds as impressions, or what the Prophet Joseph Smith referred to as "the first intimation of the spirit of revelation" or "pure intelligence flowing into you."[5]

Others, on occasion, hear an audible voice instructing and guiding them. Some are even ministered to by heavenly messengers who comfort, bless, and impart knowledge as they "speak by the power of the Holy Ghost" (2 Nephi 32:3). Many times personal revelation comes in the form of a spiritual confirmation to an answer given by an earthly source, such as the prophet or one's bishop.

Personal revelation is available to us in all aspects of our lives. Work, family, education, personal relationships, and so forth are all worthy and acceptable areas in which to seek and receive revelation. Every member of the Church also can and should receive revelation for his or her own calling. This includes stake presidents, bishops, Relief Society presidencies, home and visiting teachers, fathers and mothers, seminary class presidents. No matter the calling, the Lord has decreed a law that entitles each person who has responsibility over a stewardship to receive personal revelation relating to it.

The Prophet Joseph Smith taught, "It is also the privilege of any officer in this Church to obtain revelations, so far as it relates to his particular calling and duty in the Church. All are bound by the principles of virtue and happiness, but one great privilege of the priesthood is to obtain revelations of the mind and will of God."[6]

All members of the Church are entitled to personal revelation, and no limitation restricts the amount of revelation we can receive. The Lord has promised:

> If thou shalt ask, thou shalt receive revelation upon revelation, knowledge upon knowledge, that thou mayest know the mysteries and peaceable things—that which bringeth joy, that which bringeth life eternal. (D&C 42:61)
>
> He that keepeth his [Christ's] commandments receiveth truth and light, until he is glorified in truth and knoweth all things. (D&C 93:28)
>
> And by the power of the Holy Ghost ye may know the truth of all things. (Moroni 10:5)

One need not be a prophet or apostle to receive personal revelation about eternal truths and the mysteries of God. For example, in the Book of Mormon Jarom revealed about his people, "And there are many among us who have many revelations, for they are not all stiffnecked. And as many as are not stiffnecked and have faith, have communion with the Holy Spirit, which maketh manifest unto the children of men, according to their faith" (Jarom 1:4).

The Prophet Joseph Smith taught the principle of unlimited access to revealed truth when he declared, "God hath not revealed anything to Joseph, but what He will make known unto the Twelve, and even the least Saint may know all things as fast as he is able to bear them."[7]

Consider the following question: "Who in the Book of Mormon revealed the greatest things to the Nephites?" The answer is the children to whom Jesus ministered in 3 Nephi 26. The record states that the Savior "did teach and minister unto the children of the multitude . . . and he did loose their tongues, and they did speak unto their fathers great and marvelous things, *even greater than he had revealed unto the people*" (3 Nephi 26:14; emphasis added).

These little children received such marvelous revelation that it eclipsed even what the Savior had revealed to the multitude up to that point. This begs the question, "Why did Mormon bother to include this event without mentioning exactly what the children revealed?" At least one answer is clear: he wanted to teach the principle that revelation is available to everyone, without respect for position, gender, or age.[8] Having access to unlimited personal revelation does not mean that it is binding on the Church or that it is meant for anyone but the individual who received it. But members can—if they seek for it and are worthy—be blessed to know "all things." Church history provides us with several examples of this.

Shortly after Lorenzo Snow joined the Church, the Spirit revealed to him the principle, "As man is God once was, and as God is, man may become." He was so taken back by this profound truth and by the fact that the Lord saw fit to reveal it to him that he shared it with Brigham Young while the two were in England together on a mission. Brigham told him that the revelation was for him and him alone, and that he should not teach it as doctrine because Joseph Smith—the living prophet—had not yet done so. Brother Snow kept it strictly to himself and would not share it with another soul. Once he heard the Prophet officially reveal it, however, he felt unrestrained and could openly discuss it.[9]

Lorenzo was not the living prophet, nor even a member of the Twelve, but he received personal revelation directly from the Spirit that was not yet official Church doctrine. He clearly experienced no restriction on what he could receive, but he was restricted in what he could teach and what others were required to believe.

Similar experiences occurred a century later among many Church members who were told by the Spirit after extensive fasting and prayer that one day the priesthood would be given to all worthy males in the Church. Although it was not yet Church doctrine, they knew by personal revelation that it would be one day. After the 1978 Declaration, those who had received their insight years earlier bore testimony of what they had known by the Spirit for some time. However, many also testified that they never publicly disclosed their knowledge because they were in no position to do so. And if they had, no one else would have been under any obligation to believe or follow.

The second channel of revelation in the Church comes through the living prophet. Any revelation, instruction, guidance, directive, proclamation, or commandment to be given to the Church as a whole comes through the living prophet. Restating an earlier quotation, "Revelations of the mind and will of God to the Church, are to come through the [First] *Presidency.* This is the order of heaven, and the power and privilege of this priesthood."[10]

To clarify this principle, consider the following example. A few years ago, a stake president in Arizona received revelation that many of the members of his stake were struggling spiritually because they were neglecting their scripture study. He thought about a solution and took it to the Lord for approval. Over the next couple of weeks, he addressed the members of his stake from the pulpit of every ward and commanded them to complete a study of the Book of Mormon from beginning to end before the next stake conference. He promised them that if they did this they would experience a dramatic increase of the Spirit in their homes, in their personal lives, and would overcome the many spiritual and temporal burdens that much of the community was facing.

Happily, much of the stake obeyed their priesthood leader, and scores of testimonies were borne attesting to the fulfillment of the stake president's prophecy. But what if that stake president then sent a memo to every ward in the Church and commanded them to do the same thing? Would studying the Book of Mormon front to back be a good idea for the whole Church? Of course. Would it be within this stake president's rights to give such a directive? It absolutely would not. Nor would any other member of the Church be under any obligation to obey it aside from members of that particular stake.

In other words, the living prophet receives revelation for the whole Church. A stake president may receive revelation for his stake, and a bishop may receive revelation for his ward. A Relief Society presidency may receive revelation for their stewardship and a missionary companionship may receive revelation relating to their area. A mother and father have the right to receive revelation for their children and family. Even if a person has no official calling, every individual has the right to receive revelation for his or her own life and even has an obligation to do so. In a First Presidency message, President James E. Faust stated it this way: "Individual members, parents, and leaders have the right to receive revelation for their own responsibilities but have no duty nor right to declare the word of God beyond the limits of their own responsibilities."[11]

Personal Revelation vs. the Living Prophet

While understanding the two channels of revelation, we must understand their place in the gospel and in our personal lives. It goes without saying that each channel is indispensable to our spiritual growth, development, and salvation. We could not survive spiritually as a Church or as individual members without both vital sources of revelation. With that said, however, further clarification is needed. Of the two avenues—personal revelation through the Holy Ghost and revelation through priesthood channels under the living prophet—the latter is preeminent.

If a conflict ever arose between one's own personal revelation and what comes from the living prophet, the counsel of the prophet is paramount. This may be difficult for some, but it is nevertheless true. The living prophet has stewardship over the whole Church, including every member. Since personal revelation comes to individual members, it is governed under the direction of God's appointed representative on earth. And where a member and the prophet are in conflict, the prophet's words trump anything any other individual on earth does, says, or receives.

This does not mean that everyone who receives personal revelation that conflicts with the living prophet is necessarily wrong (although this is most often the case). It is possible for an individual to receive something from the Lord that is true and right but be in conflict with the words and teachings of the living prophet. But if that person attempts to use what he has received to challenge the Lord's appointed servant, he stands on an unsound footing.

Church history is peppered with instances where members stepped out of harmony with the Lord's living prophet over issues they knew to be true. For example, the Prophet revealed to Emma that their son, Joseph III, would succeed him in the leadership of the kingdom on earth. But when the Lord removed Joseph's family "out of their place" (D&C 93:48), Joseph revealed clearly and on several occasions that the President of the Quorum of the Twelve was to succeed him, establishing the order the Lord has required to this day.

But Emma was not satisfied with this arrangement and clung tenaciously to the earlier edict that legitimized her son's claim. Her contention was true—her husband had indeed revealed that his son would succeed him. But Emma's reliance on this truth was out of harmony with the word of the Lord later revealed through His living prophet. Rejecting the next living prophet in line, Brigham Young, only cemented her apostasy.

Over the years, I have come to learn about individuals here and there who insist on teaching or practicing things not approved by the Brethren. Most of these end up out of the Church and enemies to the living prophet. Their argument is almost always the same: the prophet is wrong because the individual has a firm basis to support a position that contradicts the prophet. Many of these people contend that they have to be right because they prayed about their beliefs or practices, and they received a confirmation that what they are doing is true and right.

But that is not what they should have been praying about. They should have prayed about whether the living prophet speaks the mind and will of God to His Church. If they had done this and truly been open to the Lord's will and to the Holy Spirit, they would have received a different answer. They would have received a confirmation that although their beliefs and practices may have a basis in truth, opposition to the living prophet makes a doctrine, practice, or belief untrue—out of harmony with the Lord. A law means nothing apart from the lawgiver. In grasping ferociously to the truth, they destroyed themselves by rejecting the truth giver. Regardless of what they had received by way of personal revelation, the word and command of the living prophet took precedence over anything they had received for themselves.

Speaking on this subject, the Prophet Joseph Smith taught:

> I will inform you that it is contrary to economy of God for any member of the Church, or any one, to receive instruction for those in authority, higher than themselves; therefore you will see the impropriety of giving heed to them; but if any person have a vision or a visitation from a heavenly messenger, it must be for his own benefit and instruction; for the fundamental principles, government, and doctrine of the Church are vested in the keys of the kingdom.[12]

President George Albert Smith testified, "There is only one pathway of safety for me in this day and that is to follow those whom the Lord has appointed to lead. I may have my own ideas and opinions. I may set up my own judgment with reference to things, but I know that when my judgment conflicts with the teachings of those that the Lord has given to us to point the way, I should change my course. If I desire salvation I will follow the leaders that our Heavenly Father has given to us."[13]

The Living Prophet Presides over Every Calling

Because revelation for the Church comes through the living prophet, it follows that revelation for any aspect of the Church also comes through the living prophet, either directly or indirectly. This means that because the prophet presides over every calling in the Church, revelation for every calling is still under the authority and direction of the living prophet. The Doctrine and Covenants reveals, "The Presidency of the High Priesthood, after the order of Melchizedek, have a right to officiate in *all the offices* in the church" (D&C 107:9; emphasis added).

A stake president, for example, may receive revelation for his stake, but it is only because he has been called though the living prophet to hold that calling and given the right to receive revelation accordingly. Even less visible callings like Sunday School teachers and ward greeters are indirectly called through the living prophet and receive their right to revelation under his direction.

Since all callings come under the direction of the living prophet, members must understand and respect two important issues. First, no Church leader is an authority unto himself. Each calling is presided over by a higher authority. For example, Relief Society presidents are subject to the leadership of a bishop. Bishops are accountable to stake presidents, stake presidents answer to Area Authorities. Area Authorities in turn report to the Area presidencies who are members of the Quorums of the Seventy. Seventies are accountable to the Quorum of the Twelve Apostles, who are subordinate to the First Presidency and ultimately the living prophet. It does not stop there. The living prophet is accountable to the Lord Jesus Christ, who obeys the will of His Father in Heaven.

Because of this hierarchy of authority, those in higher positions of responsibility are empowered to counsel and command those over whom they preside. Thus, a bishop has the right to instruct a Sunday School teacher about what he may and may not teach in his class. But what if that teacher is teaching true doctrine? Regardless of how inherently true something is, it is out of harmony if it countermands the express will of the person who has the right to set the limits and bounds of a particular practice. In this case, a bishop has the right to set the bounds of what happens in his ward.

Because every calling in the Church is extended either directly or indirectly through the living prophet and is administered under the canopy of his keys, he has an exclusive right to give any counsel or take any action he deems appropriate in relation to any member of the Church. And every member of the Church, from an apostle to the newest member, is obligated to sustain him.

The second essential issue is that because every calling in the Church is given ultimately through the living prophet, and is, therefore, an extension of his priesthood keys, members are under obligation to sustain their leaders. A Laurel needs to sustain her Young Women's president, who must in turn sustain her bishop, and so on. But remember, members are only required to sustain leaders who have stewardship over them. For example, the bishop of one ward has no authority to give direction to a member of a different ward. However, within a proper stewardship, those subordinate are under covenant to follow and sustain their leaders.

One of the wards I served in on my mission got a new bishop shortly after I arrived in the area. As one of his first acts in office, he decided to remedy the problem with noise and irreverence in the chapel following sacrament service. Each Sunday, he dismissed the congregation row by row, single file, requiring everyone to remain silent until they reached the hallway. Some ward members were disturbed by this new edict and felt such a requirement was beneath them.

But that bishop was called to preside over his ward and to give appropriate direction to his ward. The corollary of this, of course, is that the ward members, apart from their personal feelings about the man and his new direction, were under covenant to obey their bishop. Why? Because he had been called by priesthood authorities higher than himself and his calling was merely an extension of the power and authority of the living prophet. This does not mean that everyone called to a position in the Church is on par spiritually with the president of the Church; but members are required to sustain their leaders with as much commitment as they sustain the living prophet.

The Living Prophet and the World

In addition to receiving revelation for the Church and all its leaders and members, the living prophet has the right from God to receive revelation for and give commandment to the entire world. Many people, including some members of the Church, have difficulty with this doctrine, but it is nevertheless true and always has been as long as prophets have been on the earth.

Like the power and authority of God, the calling of the living prophet extends to all mankind—Latter-day Saint and not. Consider, for example, section 1 of the Doctrine and Covenants. It was dictated a year and a half after the Church was organized and after several revelations had already been received. It came later because the Lord wanted a special preface to this great book of scripture—a preface that would establish a framework for the entire book. The Lord begins by declaring:

> Hearken, O ye people of my church, saith the voice of him who dwells on high, and whose eyes are upon all men; yea, verily I say: Hearken ye people from afar; and ye that are upon the isles of the sea, listen together.
>
> For verily the voice of the Lord is unto *all men*, and there is none to escape; and there is no eye that shall not see, neither ear that shall not hear, neither heart that shall not be penetrated. . . .

> And the voice of warning shall be unto *all people*, by the mouths of my disciples, whom I have chosen in these last days. . . .
>
> Behold, this is *mine authority*, and the *authority of my servants*, and my preface unto the book of my commandments, which I have given them to publish unto you, O inhabitants of the earth. (D&C 1:1–2, 4, 6; emphasis added)

This passage establishes that the entire Doctrine and Covenants is written both to the Church *and* all the people of the world. The Lord explains His reasoning. Because this is His earth, and because sooner or later no one will escape His word or His judgment, every individual needs the opportunity to hear and accept or hear and reject His word. After all, He is concerned with all the people of the earth because they are all the children of our Father in Heaven. The Savior Himself taught that the Father "maketh his sun to rise on the evil and on the good, and sendeth rain on the just and on the unjust" (Matthew 5:45).

Although most of the inhabitants of the world are not members of the restored Church, Christ is still their Lord, their God, and their King. The scriptures testify that Christ "received all power, both in heaven and on earth" (D&C 93:17) and that He is "the Father of heaven and earth, the Creator of all things from the beginning" (Mosiah 3:8) and the "Lord of lords, and King of kings" (Revelation 17:14). Christ is all these things because "he is possessor of all things; for all things are subject unto him, both in heaven *and on the earth*" (D&C 50:27; emphasis added).

Of course, not every one will believe in God, Jesus Christ, or the restored gospel, and, therefore, not everyone will accept the living prophet. Throughout history many have rejected the prophets and their teachings. But this does not diminish the living prophet's authority to speak to the whole world. Nor does it diminish the world's responsibility to listen and obey. The Prophet Joseph Smith explained this when he taught, "The priesthood was first given to Adam: he obtained the First Presidency, and held the keys of it from generation to generation. He obtained it in the Creation, before the world was formed. . . . He had dominion given him over *every creature*."[14]

The scriptures are filled with evidences of the prophet's God-given authority over the world at large. For example, Noah commanded the world during his day to repent or they would be destroyed by flood. Everyone but his wife and his three sons and their wives ignored and persecuted him, but Noah's warnings were all fulfilled, and the world experienced firsthand the consequences of rejecting the living prophet.

When Moses was sent to Egypt to free Israel, the Lord made him "a god to Pharaoh" and told him, "Thou shalt speak all that I command thee. . . . And the Egyptians shall know that I am the Lord" (Exodus 7:1–2, 5). At that time, Egypt was the largest and most powerful nation on earth, making Pharaoh the most powerful worldly ruler. But despite all his earthly glory and might, he and his people were still subject to the God of heaven and His living prophet. The fact that Pharaoh failed to appreciate this did nothing to prevent the great Jehovah from nearly destroying Egypt with plagues and judgments.

The Lord revealed to Jeremiah that he was ordained "a prophet unto the *nations*" (Jeremiah 1:5; emphasis added) not just to Israel. The Lord sent Jonah to the wicked city of Ninevah to call them to repentance. Although the people of this city were not members of God's church, He still had authority over them, as therefore did his servant Jonah. Thankfully, they recognized Jonah's authority and repented before they were destroyed. Elisha commanded Naaman, a prominent Syrian who did not worship the God of Israel, to wash seven times in the Jordan River to be healed of leprosy. When Naaman finally humbled himself to do it, he was healed. The miracle did not necessarily come because Naaman had faith in Jehovah, but simply because he obeyed the Lord's living prophet.

The reason the heavens validate what the prophet pronounces, whether upon the Church or upon the world, is that he possesses the sealing power. The Lord explained this power to the Prophet Joseph Smith when He revealed:

> For I have conferred upon you the keys and power of the priesthood, wherein I restore all things, and make known unto you all things in due time.
>
> And verily, verily, I say unto you, that whatsoever you seal on earth shall be sealed in heaven; and whatsoever you bind on earth, in my name and by my word, saith the Lord, it shall be eternally bound in the heavens; and whosesoever sins you remit on earth shall be remitted eternally in the heavens; and whosesoever sins you retain on earth shall be retained in heaven.
>
> And again, verily I say, whomsoever you bless I will bless, and whomsoever you curse I will curse, saith the Lord; for I, the Lord, am thy God. (D&C 132:45–47)

The keys of the kingdom then, include the sealing power—the power to have things bound on earth and in heaven. And because the living prophet holds the keys of the kingdom, he has the right to the sealing power. This includes the power to perform temple marriages that last through eternity.

Consider for example the experience of Nephi II. After receiving the sealing power, he cursed the land with a famine to bring the Nephites down into humility, replacing the curse of war that the Lord had previously afflicted them with. Out of concern for the people, Nephi obtained permission from the Lord to end further bloodshed by creating a famine through the sealing power he was given. The Lord sanctioned this act and declared it binding in the presence of His angels.

It may seem reasonable that the sealing power was binding on the world in their day, but it is much more important to realize that the sealing power has no less effect in our modern day. For example, the Lord said of His authorized servants in this dispensation, "They who go forth, bearing these tidings unto the inhabitants of the earth, to them is power given to seal both on earth and in heaven, the unbelieving and the rebellious" (D&C 1:8).

This is so because they speak in the name of "the Lord who shall suddenly come to his temple; the Lord who shall come down upon the world with a curse to judgment; yea, upon *all the nations that forget God,* and upon all the ungodly among you. For he shall make bare his holy arm in the eyes of *all the nations,* and all the ends of the earth shall see the salvation of their God" (D&C 133:2–3; emphasis added).

The commandment to repent and be baptized, given so often by the prophets, applies not just to those wishing to join the Church, but to all the inhabitants of the earth. As the Lord explained, "And this revelation unto you, and commandment, is in force from this very hour upon *all the world,* and the gospel is unto all who have not received it" (D&C 84:75; emphasis added).

Consider the words of Nephi when he received a direct commandment from the Lord to the world at large. He declared boldly:

> *Hearken, O ye Gentiles,* and hear the words of Jesus Christ, the Son of the living god, which he hath commanded me that I should speak concerning you, for, behold he commandeth me that I should write saying:
>
> Turn, all ye Gentiles, from your wicked ways; and repent of your evil doings, of your lyings and deceivings, and of your whoredoms, and of your secret abominations, and your idolatries, and of your murders, and your priestcrafts, and your envyings, and your strifes, and from all

> your wickedness and abominations, and come unto me, and be baptized in my name, that ye may receive a remission of your sins, and be filled with the Holy Ghost, that ye may be numbered with my people who are of the house of Israel. (3 Nephi 30:1–2; emphasis added)

In the Doctrine and Covenants, the Lord made clear His authority over the world and His prophets' duty to command all those living on the earth. He proclaimed that "by the weak things of the earth the Lord shall thrash the nations by the power of his Spirit. And for this cause these commandments were given; they were commanded to be kept from the world in the day that they were given, but now are to go forth unto *all flesh*—And this according to the mind and will of the Lord, who ruleth over all flesh." (D&C 133:59–61; emphasis added)

If the living prophet continues to hold the keys of the kingdom and, therefore, the sealing power, there is nothing he cannot pronounce (through the will of God) and no one to whom he cannot pronounce it. But is the modern world required to believe and obey the words of the living prophet? What about presidents, kings, celebrities, or even friends and neighbors who are not of our faith? As preposterous as many people might think the principle is, the world has always been under the obligation to obey the word of the Lord given through His living prophet. Whether in ancient Egypt, ancient Jerusalem, 1830s America, or the present day, the Lord has the right to be obeyed, and He has the right to expect that His prophet will be heeded.

Perhaps some feel it unfair to place such restrictions on the world. After all, how can the Lord reasonably expect those who are not of our faith to follow the prophet and obey his words when they were not raised in the Church and have no testimony of him? However, the Lord has not left any of His children without access to His kingdom if they truly desire it. The Lord declared in the Doctrine and Covenants:

> And the Spirit giveth light to every man that cometh into the world; and the Spirit enlighteneth every man through the world, that hearkeneth to the voice of the Spirit. And everyone that hearkeneth to the voice of the Spirit cometh unto God, even the Father. And the Father teacheth him of the covenant which he has renewed . . . and not for your sakes only, but for the sake of the whole world. (D&C 84:46–48)

Because the Lord loves all the inhabitants of the earth, He has given each one a fair opportunity to find the truth. Through agency, all people can hearken to the light and continue to receive more until they find the gospel; or they limit what they receive and cut themselves off from finding and entering the kingdom. Sadly, the revelation indicates that most people do not heed the light enough to find the restored gospel, stating, "And the whole world lieth in sin, and groaneth under darkness and under the bondage of sin" (D&C 84:49).

So, requiring the world at large to heed the living prophet when they are called upon to do so is neither unfair nor unusual when one considers the Lord's authority over all mankind and the opportunities He gives to mankind to find Him and His living prophet. Therefore, the living prophet not only receives revelation to lead the Church, but he also has the God-given right to speak to the world at large, with the very real expectation that his words need to be obeyed.

Notes

1. Wilford Woodruff, *The Discourses of Wilford Woodruff,* ed. G. Homer Duram (Salt Lake City: Bookcraft, 1969), 61.
2. Joseph read the five books of Moses through the Urim and Thummim to see what parts had been deleted from the Bible. These parts were then compiled and later published in the Pearl of Great Price as the book of Moses.
3. Joseph Smith, *Teachings of the Prophet Joseph Smith,* sel. Joseph Fielding Smith (Salt Lake City: Deseret Book, 1976), 119.
4. Ibid., 328.
5. Ibid., 151.
6. Ibid., 111–12.
7. Ibid., 149.
8. See also Alma 32:23.
9. LeRoi C. Snow, "Devotion to a Divine Inspiration," *Improvement Era,* June 1919, 656.
10. Smith, *Teachings,* 111; emphasis added.
11. James E. Faust, "Continuing Revelation," *Ensign,* August 1996, 2.
12. Smith, *Teachings,* 21.
13. George Albert Smith, in Conference Reports of The Church of Jesus Christ of Latter-day Saints (Salt Lake City: The Church of Jesus Christ of Latter-day Saints, 1898 to present), April 1937, 33.
14. Smith, *Teachings,* 157; emphasis added.

CHAPTER THREE

Principle 2: The Living Prophet Is the Only Person Who Can Receive Revelation for the Church

Revelation for the Church requires a living prophet. However, he is not only empowered to receive revelation, but he also is the only person on earth at a given time who is authorized to receive revelation for the Church—that is, for the *entire* Church.

Many great minds and noble souls have graced the Church in these latter days. Some were marvelous scriptorians, others were masterful teachers, many had exceptional spiritual gifts, while still others distinguished themselves through scholarship and academic achievement. All of these have made a difference in the Church through their service and contributions; and they have no doubt taught many Church members much about the truths of the kingdom and the doctrines of eternity. But no matter how much they have learned or taught, no matter how much insight they have gained over the years, no matter how pure their desire to serve the Lord Jesus Christ, only the living prophet has ever been authorized to receive revelation for the entire Church.

Teaching this principle to the elders of the Church, the Lord declared in section 107, "And again, the duty of the President of the office of the

High Priesthood is to preside over the whole church, and to be like unto Moses—behold, here is wisdom; yea, to be a seer, a revelator, a translator, and a prophet, having all the gifts of God which he bestows upon the head of the church" (D&C 107:91–92).

This doctrine is reiterated in section 132. Speaking of the laws pertaining to the new and everlasting covenant (eternal marriage and so much more), the Lord stated, "I have appointed unto my servant Joseph to hold this power in the last days, and there is *never but one on earth at a time* on whom this power and the keys of this priesthood are conferred" (D&C 132:7; emphasis added).

Early Church history provides a remarkable example of this principle in action. In 1830, a few months after the Church was organized, Hiram Page, one of the Eight Witnesses to the Book of Mormon, came into possession of a special stone from which he claimed to receive revelation and direction from the Lord concerning the restored Church. His claim was so extraordinary, in fact, that some members began following him and obeying his new directives rather than heeding the Prophet Joseph Smith.

Even Oliver Cowdery—the Second Elder of the Church—was deceived by what became known as Hiram Page's "peep stone." Concerned about the small but growing apostasy, the Prophet Joseph Smith sought direction from the Lord on the matter just prior to meeting with the Saints at a Church conference in September 1830. This inquiry resulted in section 28 of the Doctrine and Covenants. In it the Lord declared:

> Behold, I say unto thee, Oliver, that it shall be given unto thee that thou shalt be heard by the church in all things whatsoever thou shalt teach them by the Comforter, concerning the revelations and commandments which I have given.
>
> But, behold, verily, verily, I say unto thee, *no one* shall be appointed to receive commandments and revelations in this church excepting my servant Joseph Smith, Jun., for he receiveth them even as Moses.
>
> And thou shalt be obedient unto the things which I shall give unto him, even as Aaron, to declare faithfully the commandments and revelations, with power and authority unto the church. (D&C 28:1–3; emphasis added)

In these few verses, the Lord gave clear and unequivocal instruction to Oliver about how revelation flows to His Church. He acknowledged Oliver's role as a counselor to the Prophet Joseph and a teacher and leader to the Saints, but the Prophet Joseph alone was authorized to receive revelation, counsel, commandments, and doctrine for the Church as a whole. In fact, the Lord patiently reminded Oliver in the first verse that he should be heard by Church members when he should teach them about the revelations that had already been given through the living prophet and that he should teach by the Spirit.

The Lord's analogy to Moses and Aaron is a fascinating one. He likens the Prophet Joseph Smith's position and authority to that of Moses anciently. Moses was the Lord's living prophet and was chosen to speak for Him in all things, having been given exclusive authority to do so for all the world in his day. Aaron was given authority to act as a revelator and spokesman for his brother Moses. He was to serve Moses as a subordinate and counselor. Similarly, Oliver was appointed Second Elder of the Church—not for his own glory but for the glory of God and the benefit of the Prophet, to act as his spokesman and counselor.

In Moses' day, Aaron found his way into apostasy when his prophet-brother was atop Mt. Sinai communing with Jehovah. Aaron took it upon himself to lead Israel on his own authority with disastrous results. A golden calf was built, many forsook their God, and a nation roamed the desert for forty years. Although Oliver's lapse in judgment failed to match the seriousness of Aaron's, and though the situation with Hiram Page's peep stone did not have quite the tragic result the golden calf did, the Lord used Oliver's mistake to give valuable instruction about how revelation works in His kingdom.

As for Hiram Page's unique stone, it turned out that he truly was receiving revelations and commandments; but tragically, he was receiving them from the wrong source. The Lord explained this to the Prophet and instructed him on how to deal with his wayward friend. He told him to direct Oliver to "take thy brother, Hiram Page . . . and tell him that those things which he hath written from that stone are not of me and that Satan deceiveth him; For, behold, these things have not been appointed unto him, neither shall anything be appointed unto *any* of this church contrary to the church covenants" (D&C 28:11–12; emphasis added).

Once again, the Lord explained to Hiram Page, and to all the Saints, that no one but His authorized living prophet had the right to speak for Him to the whole Church. And the corollary is, therefore, true: the Saints are under covenant as members of Christ's Church to heed that which is given or sanctioned by His living prophet.

The Doctrine and Covenants provides us with other clear references to the principle that the living prophet is the only person authorized by the Lord to receive revelation and give commandment for the whole Church. In response to false claims by some misguided members that they were receiving authorized revelations for the Church, the Lord asserted in section 43:

> For behold, verily, verily, I say unto you, that ye have received a commandment for a law unto my church, through him whom I have appointed unto you to receive commandments and revelations from my hand.
>
> And this ye shall know assuredly—that there is *none other* appointed unto you to receive commandments and revelations until he be taken, if he abide in me.
>
> But verily, verily, I say unto you, that *none else* shall be appointed unto this gift except it be through him . . .
>
> And this shall be a law unto you, that ye receive not the teachings of any that shall come before you as revelations or commandments;
>
> And this I give unto you that you may not be deceived, that you may know they are not of me. (D&C 43:2–6; emphasis added)

What a straightforward, unequivocal statement. The Lord first confirms that He appointed Joseph Smith to be a prophet and revelator to the Saints to receive revelation directly from His hand. Then, the Saints are told explicitly that the prophet is the *only* person authorized to receive on behalf of the whole Church so long as he lives and is faithful. The revelation continues by asserting that no one else may receive anything for the Church unless it is under the direction of the prophet. To conclude, the Lord states plainly that anything given to the body of the Church by anyone other than the living prophet (or those he has authorized) is not to be considered official doctrine or commandment; those receiving such teachings are being deceived.

Confirming this order of leadership, President George Q. Cannon stated that when God organized His Church, He gave "to one man, and to one man only, at a time, the keys to preside over and to communicate the mind and will of God to that Church. While that man is in that position, seeking to magnify it, He [God] will not speak to other men and give them revelations for His Church." According to President Cannon, even though every member is entitled to revelation, "that does not give them the right to give revelations to the Church. God did not design it. God never has warranted or sustained any such action."[1]

Priesthood Keys

The prophet has the exclusive right to direct the Church because he holds the proper priesthood keys. The priesthood is the authority to act in the name of God, and priesthood keys constitute the right to use that authority in certain ways. In other words, each calling or position in the kingdom of God carries certain duties and responsibilities. Each of these callings constitutes a stewardship—the care of a particular assignment—and is accompanied by the keys to direct and administer that calling.

For example, a nineteen-year-old missionary has the same priesthood authority as a ward elders quorum president. However, just because they have equal authority (they are both elders in the Melchizedek Priesthood), they don't have the right to use their authority in the same way. The missionary would be out of line if he attempted to rearrange the home teaching schedule, and, by the same token, the elders quorum president would have no right to baptize his friend without approval from the full-time missionaries. One holds keys to direct a quorum of elders in a ward while the other holds keys to preside over all missionary work in an assigned area. Yet both hold the same priesthood authority.

The reason the living prophet is the only person who has the right to preside over the whole Church is that he holds *all* the keys that are given on earth at a particular time. No one on earth holds any keys that are not held by the living prophet, and anyone holding any keys does so under the direction of, and is subordinate to, the living prophet. He has the right to preside over the affairs of every calling, position, and stewardship. Section 107 of the Doctrine and Covenants reveals, "The power and authority of the higher, or Melchizedek Priesthood, is to hold the keys of all the spiritual blessings of the church. . . . And again, the duty of the President of the office the High Priesthood is to preside over the whole church, and to be like unto Moses . . . yea to be a seer, a revelator, a translator, and a prophet, having all the gifts of God which he bestows upon the head of the Church" (D&C 107:18, 91–92).

President James E. Faust further clarified this relationship when he wrote, "The greatest revelator in our time has been Joseph Smith. . . . Each of the 92 apostles called since then has been sustained as a prophet, seer, and revelator. But the prophets, seers, and revelators succeeding Joseph as *Presidents of the Church* have been those apostles in whom all of the keys of Christ's earthly kingdom have been active and functioning."[2]

President Joseph F. Smith also reinforced this principle to the Church, stating, "Every act performed under [priesthood] authority shall be done at the proper time and place, in the proper way, and after the proper order. The power of directing these labors constitutes the keys of the Priesthood." Continuing, he explained that in their fulness, "the keys are held by only one person at a time, the prophet and president of the Church. He may delegate any portion of this power to another, in which case that person holds the keys of that particular labor. Thus, the president of a temple, the president of a stake, the bishop of a ward, the president of a mission, the president of a quorum, each hold the keys of their particular assignments. But the priesthood they hold does not increase by their special appointment."[3]

Other Church Leaders

The Lord has called other men and women to lead the Church, such as General Authorities and general presidencies, but these men and women operate under the direction of the living prophet. Some members find it easier to listen to and follow certain leaders because they feel a special affinity or kinship with them. And although it is appropriate and normal to identify with some of the brethren or even certain sisters more than others or be influenced in a special way by them, this must not distract us from looking to the living prophet as the one and only ultimate authority on earth.

Notes

1. George Q. Cannon, in *Journal of Discourses,* 26 vols. (London: Latter-day Saints' Book Depot, 1854–86), 26:63–64.
2. James E. Faust, "Continuing Revelation," *Ensign,* August 1996, 2; emphasis added.
3. Joseph F. Smith, *Gospel Doctrine: Selections from the Sermons and Writings of Joseph F. Smith* (Salt Lake City: Deseret Book, 1971), 136.

CHAPTER FOUR

Principle 3: The Living Prophet Is Authorized to Give Revelation and Commandment on Any Subject

I once heard a Sunday School teacher ask his class the following question: "What does the prophet have the right to give counsel about?" Immediately, nearly everyone in the class exclaimed (almost in unison) "*Anything*!" But one very different answer echoed from the back of the room: "Only those things that specifically apply to the Church!" When asked to clarify his answer, the brother who made the comment explained that it was his understanding that God raised up prophets to give us guidance and direction about "Church matters" and "spiritual things" and that counsel and advice about other areas could easily be obtained from individuals who have spent their lives becoming expert in their particular fields of learning and knowledge.

When questioned further about his perspective, this particular brother expressed the opinion that the prophet has spent years of his life training for spiritual or Church matters, so he is the person to seek out on those issues. And by the same logic, questions concerning other areas ought to be left to those in the world who have spent their time studying their unique fields of interest. He summed up his argument, attempting to put the whole matter to rest, by stating, "The prophet is just too busy running the Church. . . . It's not his job to get involved with other things."

After listening to this class member, I don't believe he intended any harm. His reasoning lay more in ignorance than apostasy. He truly believed that the prophet's role was confined to what he referred to as "spiritual matters." Surprisingly, this perspective is not completely unfamiliar in the Church. As odd as it may seem, some members profess to believe in the calling of the living prophet, yet attempt to place their own limits on his authority. By this I mean they accept the prophet's right to receive revelation for and give commandment to the Saints on "spiritual" matters but argue that he has no right to overstep his bounds and make declarations in any other area.

This attitude reveals three serious errors in judgment. First, it reveals a lack of faith in the Lord God and His omniscience; second, it stems from the belief that the living prophet acts on his own accord instead of under the direction of Jesus Christ; third, it assumes the Lord makes a fundamental distinction between spiritual and temporal matters.

God's Omniscience

The first and most obvious problem with believing the prophet has limits on what he may or may not speak about is that it reveals an alarming lack of faith in the omniscience of God. Perhaps the chief reason some members of the Church feel justified in criticizing the living prophet for giving counsel apart from mere "spiritual" matters is that they don't feel he has the training and expertise in certain areas to form an appropriate opinion. What these people fail to recognize is that the prophet is not the individual giving the directive; he is only the Lord's mouthpiece.

But is the Lord's knowledge broad enough for us to have complete confidence in His ability to command in all things? The scriptures provide a more than adequate answer. For example, the Book of Mormon declares:

> O how great the holiness of our God! For he knoweth *all things,* and there is not anything save he knows it (2 Nephi 9:20; emphasis added).
>
> My joy is carried away, even unto boasting in my God; for he has all power, all wisdom, and all understanding; he comprehendeth *all things* (Alma 26:35; emphasis added).

Other scriptures state:

> He comprehendeth *all things*, and all things are before him, and all things are round about him; and he is above all things, and in all things, and is through all things, and is round about all things; and all things are by him, and of him, even God, forever and ever (D&C 88:41; emphasis added).
>
> There is no God beside me, and *all things* are present with me, for I know them all (Moses 1:6; emphasis added).

If God is omniscient—if he knows, comprehends, and discerns all things in the universe in a single moment—there would be no way or need to place a limit on what He can and cannot (or should and should not) reveal to His children. Indeed, if the Lord is all knowing, how could He be in error at any time, regardless of the subject or circumstance? Is it possible the Lord is unfamiliar with law or politics? Could he be ignorant of some aspects of medicine or physics? Does psychology, sociology, or literature escape His grasp? Is he impaired by language, culture, or societal barriers?

The plain and immutable truth is that God knows all things, and nothing can be hidden from His understanding. With this in mind, it is reasonable to assume that if God gives direction on a given subject, regardless of what it is, He knows why it is necessary and why we need to follow it.

The Prophet or the Lord

When the Lord gives direction or counsel on a given subject, it is necessary and right to follow it because it is based on His infinite wisdom. Since this is true, the corollary is therefore also true: when that direction comes through a prophet on earth, it is equally necessary and right. To say it a different way, just because God reveals something through His prophet doesn't mean it is less true or less important or that God doesn't still ultimately understand what He is doing and why He is doing it.

Perhaps if the prophet spoke of his own accord, based on his own wisdom, one might find grounds to doubt, to murmur, to criticize. But the prophet is merely a servant, a messenger, a conduit through which the Lord reveals His will. When the prophet speaks on behalf of the Lord, the direction transcends earthly, human wisdom and belongs instead to God's realm of knowledge and understanding—a realm that is infinite and not fully comprehensible to the frail minds of men.

Many of God's covenant people (and for that matter the world at large) have taken it upon themselves to criticize the living prophet for particular counsel or commandments they either do not appreciate or they disagree with. Many of them argue that these directives are merely the prophet's opinions and that he must be in error for some reason or another. Some attack counsel based on the prophet's personality, his political ideals, his education, his lack of worldly expertise in a given area, or simply some personal human frailty.

All of these attacks boil down to one argument: *the prophet as a man is imperfect and, therefore, his counsel must be faulty.* It is interesting to observe that people who take this position only do so when they personally disagree with a given directive. They are more than happy to sustain the prophet when the counsel or commandment does not conflict with their personal opinions or preferences.

But the prophet's calling has nothing to do with his strengths or weaknesses. He is not called because he is perfect or because everyone agrees with his words and commandments. He is called for one reason and one reason only: the Lord God wants him to be the prophet. In fact, the Lord calls prophets (as he calls all of us) *in spite* of their weaknesses. Rather than diminishing the validity of a prophet's words, it makes them all the more credible. Think of it—commandments, counsel, and directions that have proven to be right and true throughout the years were given by the Lord through imperfect men. If they could get it right while still imperfect, prophets can and will continue to get it right because their revelation comes from the same source it always has—the God of Heaven.

If we would examine the life of the prophets throughout history, I believe we would find that almost all of them had some weakness that seemed to them or others to inhibit their ability to serve as the Lord's representatives. For example, during the translation of the Book of Mormon, Oliver Cowdery pointed out the Prophet Joseph Smith's deficiencies with the English language. In fact, he remarked that Joseph could not spell the word "February" without using the Urim and Thummim.[1] Moses and Enoch were "slow of speech" (Moses 6:31), Nephi had no idea how to build a ship, and Moroni lamented over his weaknesses with writing. And yet, the Lord chose them according to His foreknowledge, prepared them, called them, and sustained them in that calling.

The reason the Lord did all these things for His prophets is stunningly clear—the work they were called to perform was His, and when the Lord calls someone to a work, He qualifies them for it. When we as mortals compare ourselves to the Lord, we find that we are all hopelessly lost without His power and direction. Compared to His knowledge, power, glory, and abilities, every person—from the accomplished professor to the simple child—is hopelessly incapable of rendering any useful service to the Lord without His help. However, with the Lord we all have the power to do everything the Lord would have us do. As Nephi testified, "I know that the Lord giveth no commandments unto the children of men, save he shall prepare a way for them that they may accomplish the thing which he commandeth them" (1 Nephi 3:7).

Perhaps this point can be further illustrated by a practical example. When the Word of Wisdom was first given to the Church, it engendered ridicule and opposition. Because they had no real medical training, the Prophet and other Church leaders were mocked by the so-called experts of the day. Relying on the world's best scientific thinking, many of these experts made outrageous claims, such as tobacco actually promoted respiratory health or that reducing red meat in one's diet weakened the body. Of course, anyone with access to even the most limited medical sources today is aware of the dangers of substances like alcohol, tobacco, coffee and tea, and the benefits of a moderate diet of whole grains, fruits, vegetables, and limited meat.

What is the difference between the nineteenth century and today? Did the substances mentioned in section 89 of the Doctrine and Covenants suddenly change their properties? Has man's physiology mutated so dramatically in less than two hundred years? Of course not. Nothing changed between then and now except that the understanding of men is approaching a point where medical experts are discovering what God knew all along. In other words, scientists are realizing what the Lord's prophet, with no formal medical training, revealed nearly two centuries before. The Prophet Joseph Smith said it best: "Whatever God requires is right, no matter what it is, although we may not see the reason thereof until long after the events transpire."[2]

Every Latter-day Saint who confesses to have a testimony of the restored gospel must come to accept the fundamental and very simple truth that prophets get their direction to speak from God Himself, and they have the right and expertise to speak on any subject at any time because they are not relying upon their own limited knowledge but upon God's direction, guidance, and living revelation. Surely the Lord God will do nothing but He revealeth His secret unto His servants the prophets;

and surely his servants will do nothing but they receive those revelations first from the Lord God!

Spiritual vs. Temporal

A third problem with the belief that the prophet should only speak on "spiritual" or Church issues is that it assumes there is a difference between spiritual matters and all others. It assumes the Lord makes a distinction between "spiritual" and temporal issues[3] and that the Lord only concerns Himself, and therefore His prophet, with things directly related to the operations of the Church. However, The Lord has revealed the exact opposite. For example, He has taught the Saints:

> Wherefore, verily I say unto you that *all things* unto me are *spiritual*, and not at any time have I given unto you a law which was temporal; neither any man, nor the children of men; neither Adam, your father, whom I created.
>
> Behold, I gave unto him that he should be an agent unto himself; and I gave unto him commandment, but no temporal commandment gave I unto him, for my commandments are spiritual; they are not natural nor temporal, neither carnal nor sensual. (D&C 29:34–35; emphasis added)

It appears that some of the early Saints of this dispensation had quite a difficult time reconciling the spiritual and the temporal in one. The Lord had to give clarification several times on this issue. For example, section 107 of the Doctrine and Covenants reveals, "A high priest, that is, after the order of Melchizedek, may be set apart unto the ministering of *temporal things*, having a knowledge of them by the Spirit of truth" (D&C 107:71; emphasis added).

President Brigham Young also spoke about the unfounded difference some people make between spiritual and temporal matters. He stated that some Church leaders in Kirtland "were much opposed to Joseph the Prophet, meddling with temporal affairs." In a public meeting he told the Saints, "Ye Elders of Israel . . . will some of you draw the line of demarcation between the spiritual and temporal in the kingdom of God, so that I may understand it?" When not one of them could do so, he defied "any man on earth to point out his duty, and just how far he must go, in dictating temporal or spiritual things. Temporal and spiritual things are inseparably connected, and ever will be."[4]

President George Q. Cannon taught the same principle, explaining,

"There is an authority in the Church to whom God has given the right to counsel . . . in regard to temporal affairs. When Joseph Smith lived upon the earth it was his prerogative to do that . . . and on his departure another took his place upon the earth. That was Brigham Young. When he passed away another stepped forward . . . and exercises the same authority."[5] Supporting this precept, President Wilford Woodruff stated, "Our President has frequently told us that we cannot separate the temporal from the spiritual, but they must go hand in hand together, and so it is, and so must we act in reference to building up the kingdom of God."[6]

Why do people want to separate the spiritual from the temporal? For some, it is because they accept being commanded in Church matters but want to conduct other areas of their lives according to the world's standards. Are these people truly seeking to build Zion or only attempting to serve both "God and mammon" (Matthew 6:24)?

Perhaps others think that God is not concerned about what goes on in the world generally and is only interested in Church affairs. The Lord addressed this kind of thinking in the Doctrine and Covenants. In one such instance He commands:

> Teach ye diligently and my grace shall attend you, that you may be instructed more perfectly in theory, in principle, in doctrine, in the law of the gospel, in *all things* that pertain unto the kingdom of God, that are expedient for you to understand;
>
> Of things both in heaven and in the earth, and under the earth; things which have been, things which are, things which must shortly come to pass; things which are at home, things which are abroad; the wars and the perplexities of the nations, and the judgments which are on the land; and a knowledge also of countries and of kingdoms. (D&C 88:78–79; emphasis added)

In section 90, the Lord reveals that we must "study and learn, and become acquainted with all good books, and with languages, tongues, and people" (D&C 90:15). He also commands, "Hasten to . . . obtain a knowledge of history, and of countries, and of kingdoms, of laws of God and man, and all this for the salvation of Zion" (D&C 93:53).

In these stunning revelations the Lord tells us clearly that a knowledge of what appear to be temporal concerns, such as history, literature, politics, international relations, geography, languages, law, and many other subjects all pertain directly to the kingdom of God. Obviously, the Lord makes no distinction between the spiritual and the temporal when dealing with the world He created. And because of this, neither He nor any of His prophets need to be confined to what some consider strictly spiritual matters. Remember, according to the Lord Himself, "all things unto me are spiritual" (D&C 29:34).

Expertise of the World

In addition to pouring out knowledge and truth upon the Latter-day Saints, the Lord also blesses the world in general with learning and wisdom to gain expertise in various fields of study. Indeed, the Lord has poured out light and knowledge to all His children throughout the world, and more people than ever before now have access to education and opportunities that advance them in diverse careers and fields. It is appropriate to take advantage of what others have learned, whether they are LDS or not; to not do so would forfeit great opportunity and blessings. As the Prophet Joseph Smith taught, "One of the grand fundamental principles of 'Mormonism' is to receive truth, let it come from whence it may."[7]

Notwithstanding the tremendous advantages we can receive from looking to the experts of the world, we must be very careful not to be misled by false teachings, diligently seeking to discern between truth and error. Year after year the experts of the world reject more and more gospel principles and attempt to replace eternal truths with the philosophies of men. Moreover, those who hold fast to gospel truths in the face of some so-called worldly expertise are ridiculed and mocked. However, the Lord has foretold what will happen to those who base their learning on false precepts. Speaking of the faithful who rely on Him, the Lord declared, "And their wisdom shall be great, and their understanding reach to heaven; and before them the wisdom of the wise shall perish, and the understanding of the prudent shall come to naught" (D&C 76:9).

The living prophet is authorized speak to the Church as a whole, to individual members, or to the world in general on any subject at any time. And if he does so, we are obligated by covenant to sustain, follow, and obey as if the Lord Himself had appeared to us personally with the same message. The essential question each of us needs to ask is, "Do I have faith in God, and do I have faith in His living prophet?"

Notes

1. A reference made by Martin Harris (document contained in the Church Historical Department).
2. Joseph Smith, *Teachings of the Prophet Joseph Smith,* sel. Joseph Fielding Smith

(Salt Lake City: Deseret Book, 1976), 256.

3. Some scriptures make a distinction between the spiritual and the temporal, but they do so only to differentiate importance and duration in the eternal scheme. However, they reveal that both are under the direction and power of God, who knows all things and who gives counsel to His prophet on what to reveal to the world, both spiritual and temporal.
4. Brigham Young, in *Journal of Discourses,* 26 vols. (London: Latter-day Saints' Book Depot, 1854–86), 10:363–64.
5. George Q. Cannon, in *Journal of Discourses*, 4:274.
6. Wilford Woodruff, in *Journal of Discourses*, 9:325.
7. Smith, *Teachings,* 313.

CHAPTER FIVE

Principle 4: The Living Prophet Is Only a Prophet When He Speaks As a Prophet

Chapter 4 established the principle that the living prophet can and does speak on any subject the Lord sees fit to reveal. Whatever comes out of the mouth of the living prophet while he is acting by the keys of his calling is doctrine and commandment and needs to be obeyed in order to receive certain blessings. While this principle is true and remains a standard by which faithfulness is measured, this chapter will introduce a principle that somewhat amends the previous one. By amends I mean simply that while it is necessary to observe and obey all the words a prophet speaks under the direction of the Lord, we are not necessarily required to follow or even believe *all* the words a prophet speaks.

Before any assumptions are made, clarification needs to be made. Unquestionably, we must sustain the living prophet and work to obey those commandments he gives and believe those truths he reveals. But it is possible for well-intentioned persons to take this to the extreme. Some have assumed, for example, that *every* word that comes out of the prophet's mouth is doctrine, commandment, and absolute truth, and must be followed without question or hesitation.

In following and sustaining the prophet, it would appear that we are faced with a contradiction. On the one hand, we are required by covenant to follow the prophet's words regardless of our own desires or opinions. On the other hand, we are required by that same covenant to be somewhat choosy and are not obligated to believe or follow everything that comes out of the prophet's mouth. How is this so? There is a distinction between the prophet as a man and the prophet speaking under his calling. The Prophet Joseph Smith put it more plainly. He once recorded in a journal entry: "This morning I read German and visited with a brother and sister from Michigan, who thought that 'a prophet is always a prophet;' but I told them that a prophet was a prophet only when he was acting as such."[1]

What did the Prophet mean by the statement that a prophet is only a prophet "when he was acting as such"? He meant that prophets are human beings, who are imperfect and subject to weakness like every other human being. Even though they are better than most men because they have given themselves to the Lord in great prayer, sacrifice, and righteous living, they still make mistakes and sometimes have opinions that may not be the express will of the Lord. In other words, they are not all-knowing and all-powerful as the Lord Himself is. Because of this, they have the ability to act or speak on a personal level in ways that are imperfect.

The Prophet Joseph Smith admitted this of himself on more than one occasion. For example, after being criticized by some of the Saints for perceived shortcomings, he admitted, "I told them that I was but a man, and they must not expect me to be perfect; if they expected perfection from me, I should expect it from them; but if they would bear with my infirmities and the infirmities of the brethren, I would likewise bear with their infirmities."[2]

What those few critical Saints failed to realize, however, was that although the Prophet humbly and lovingly admitted his imperfections, he was not guilty of the offenses they accused him of. Making a distinction between his weaknesses as a man and his performance as the Lord's prophet, he firmly clarified, "Although I do wrong, I do not the wrongs that I am charged with doing; the wrong that I do is through the frailty of human nature, like other men. No man lives without fault."[3] Just because living prophets are men does not mean in any way that when they speak in the name of the Lord they are subject to mistakes. It simply means that a prophet does not speak in the name of the Lord every second of the day.

Prophets Are Men

No servant of the Lord Jesus Christ has ever been perfect while laboring on the earth; this includes the prophets—even Presidents of the Church! As difficult as it may be for some to believe, prophets are men with frailties, weaknesses, annoying habits, quirks, and everyday human struggles. They are men raised up by the Lord to do a job they could never do on their own because they simply aren't capable of it. That is not to say that they are not good men with many great abilities, but the fact remains that no one is capable of representing the Lord without His guidance, direction, and sustaining power.

Consider the words of some of the prophets throughout history who have been called by the Lord. Each one of them recognized all too clearly how profoundly unprepared and unequal to the task they were. For example, Enoch, the great priest and king whose city stood alone against the darkness of the world, asked the Lord, "Why is it that I have found favor in thy sight, and am but a lad, and all the people hate me; for I am slow of speech; wherefore am I thy servant?" (Moses 6:31).

When the Lord first appeared to Moses and commanded him to free Israel from Egypt, Moses was "afraid to look upon God" (Exodus 3:6) and then asked the great Jehovah, "Who am I . . . that I should bring forth the children of Israel out of Egypt?" (Exodus 3:11). When Isaiah was called to perform his holy task, rather than rejoicing he exclaimed, "Woe is me! for I am undone; because I am a man of unclean lips, and I dwell in the midst of a people with unclean lips" (Isaiah 6:5). Amos recounted his unexpected calling and declared, "I was no prophet, neither was I a prophet's son; but I was an herdman, and a gatherer" (Amos 7:14). Nephi and Moroni both lamented their weakness in writing (2 Nephi 33:1; Ether 12:23, 40), and the Doctrine and Covenants contains more than one instance of the Prophet Joseph Smith's imperfections, including losing 116 original pages of the Book of Mormon manuscript.

No prophet has ever been perfect or infallible; each one has made mistakes, labored with weakness, and has been afflicted by simple human nature, or what King Benjamin called the "natural man" (Mosiah 3:19). And, yet, the miracle is that God Himself has seen fit in His infinite wisdom and love to call these imperfect men in spite of themselves. For example, trying to teach this principle to Sidney Rigdon, the Lord declared in a revelation, "And I have sent forth the fulness of my gospel by the hand of my servant Joseph; and in weakness I have blessed him" (D&C 35:17).

What makes this fact even more remarkable is that the Lord also does the same for each and every one of us. Which member of the Church has ever qualified for a particular blessing or even a Church calling without the love, mercy, and sustaining hand of the Lord Jesus Christ? (In case I'm not making my point very well here, the answer is *no one*). This precept is most profoundly expressed in the book of Ether. The Lord explains, "And if men come unto me I will show unto them their weakness. I give unto men weakness that they may be humble; and my grace is sufficient for all men that humble themselves before me; for if they humble themselves before me, and have faith in me, then will I make weak things become strong unto them" (Ether 12:27).

Having established that prophets are mortal and imperfect men, it is safe to assume that they sometimes make mistakes in their personal lives. And even if they do not make an outright mistake, their personal wisdom is still limited. We as Saints of Christ's Church must understand that although we are obligated by a covenant made of our own free will to follow the living prophet, we are not obligated to follow the man. We are not required by God or Church leaders to obey the counsel or believe a teaching of any prophet if he is not speaking as the prophet but merely expressing his own personal opinion.

Would you tell your children not to eat their vegetables just because the living prophet remarked that he did not care for vegetables? Would it be rational to expect every Church member to give up reading novels if the living prophet commented that he disliked reading fiction? By the same token, a statement or publication of the living prophet made years before he became the president of the Church does not necessarily constitute doctrine, and members would not be obligated to believe or obey it. Of course, this does not mean the opinions or writings are untrue; the Saints are simply are not obligated by covenant to accept such things.

Remember, the Lord requires us to observe all the prophet's words "as *he* receiveth them, walking in all holiness before me" (D&C 21:4).

In other words, we are obligated to obey only when the prophet has first received the direction from the Lord. If it is not given or sanctioned by the Lord to the office of president of the Church, no matter how good or true it is, we are not under covenant to obey.

Years ago, a friend of mine (who is related to one of our past Church presidents) attended a family reunion that the prophet attended. While she was in a private room of the house tending to her baby, the President received a phone call from Church headquarters. Needing some privacy to talk, he was shown by the owner of the house to the room where my friend was looking after her child. Not wanting to intrude or rush a nursing mother, the prophet patiently waited a few moments for my friend to finish up and leave before he took the call. As she prepared to exit, he went out of his way to compliment her on a particular practice of childcare. He explained why he felt it was so beneficial for both mother and child and expressed his gratitude for her as a mother and nurturer.

When she relayed the account of her brush with the prophet to me, I asked her if he had commanded her to continue the practice or if he just expressed his personal feelings. It was obvious that she had never considered that question before. But after thinking a few moments, she stated that she felt no real counsel or command had been given, he was just expressing his opinion. She added that she wasn't concerned whether it was commandment or not because she held the prophet as a person in enough esteem that she would continue caring for all her children the way he suggested.

The comments made by the prophet were almost assuredly not official counsel or commandment. They were, nevertheless, probably good advice based on years of experience, wisdom, and a deep gospel perspective. And although my friend felt she should follow the advice of the prophet, the man, she was under no *obligation* to follow or obey because the comments were not expressed by the prophet through the keys of his calling. Even if he expressed them as he was inspired by the Holy Ghost, he gave the direction to my friend alone and not to anyone else at that time. Hearing this account, I, for example, was under no obligation to follow the advice he gave because it was not given to me personally or to the Church membership in general.

How Will You Know?

How can one tell when a prophet's words are binding on the Church? Most of the time it's obvious. First, any revelation received by the living prophet and contained in the scriptures is doctrine and the word of the Lord. This includes the Doctrine and Covenants. Second, when the prophet gives an address in an official capacity, such as during general conference, his words are binding on the Church. Third, when the prophet's words are printed in Church publications like the *Ensign,* they are similarly binding. The prophet also occasionally sends directives to Church leadership and general Church membership, which also require adherence. Of course, anything the prophet proclaims to the world is binding upon nonmembers, such as "The Family: A Proclamation to the World," or "The Living Christ: The Testimony of the Apostles."

Confidence in the Living Prophet As a Man

Having established the idea that the prophet does not always speak as a prophet, fair warning needs to be given. The living prophet has been called to his position for good reason. He knows enough about the gospel and has proven his commitment to the Lord sufficient that he is a man whom the Lord can trust. And if the Lord can trust a man's character, intelligence, righteousness, and integrity enough to make that man His representative, we as Saints need to be equally trusting—and then some. When the prophet speaks as a man and makes mistakes, they usually involve trivial matters that do not affect the course of our lives one way or the other. But most of the time when he speaks as a man, his opinion is at least worth serious consideration. When an individual has spent his life in solemn service to the Lord, has been affiliated with some of the finest men of the day, has had thorough experience with all facets of Church leadership, has had spiritual experiences beyond most mortal men, and has an intimate relationship with the God of Heaven, there is a good chance his perspective might be solid enough to form valid opinions about a great many things.

I once overheard a member of the Church speaking to a former General Authority about Church doctrine. The member was interrogating his patient listener about early Church leaders and their teachings, expressing his confusion and disapproval. When the former General Authority asked the man what his exact problem was, he replied that he had the most difficulty with many of Brigham Young's teachings as recorded in the *Journal of Discourses.* He argued that because the multi-volume work was not officially published by the Church, the Prophet's teachings were not considered doctrine. "Brigham Young did a lot of speculating!" exclaimed the distraught brother.

Kindly, the former General Authority retorted, "Maybe Brigham was speculating. But he was the foremost student of Joseph Smith, an Apostle, one of only a handful of leaders at Kirtland who never turned on Joseph, the organizer and leader of the exodus west, the greatest American colonizer, Governor of the Utah Territory, and prophet and President of the Church. . . . I'll take Brigham's speculation over almost anyone else's doctrine."

The point here is that when we realize how extraordinary the living prophets are and how highly the Lord thinks of them, we will be less concerned about whether the prophet is expressing his opinion and more concerned about learning all we can from an amazing man. This does not mean we have to like his personality, nor are we bound to obey when he speaks on his own accord. But with such a lack of true leadership in the world, the words of the prophet, even if only spoken as a man, should be as precious as gold to us.

The Prophet's Calling

Prophets can indeed be imperfect when acting as men. However, the other side of the issue needs to be addressed plainly and without misunderstanding. When the living prophet is not acting or speaking as a man, he is doing so by the keys of his calling. When he does this—when he pronounces, admonishes, and commands under the direction of the Lord—he is no longer to be considered just an imperfect man, and we are obligated to believe, follow, and obey. As President Brigham Young explained it, "I have never yet preached a sermon and sent it out to the children of men, that they may not call scripture."[4]

Speaking of the difference between the man and the calling, President George Q. Cannon stated, "Now was not Joseph Smith a mortal man? Yes. A fallible man? Yes. Had he not weaknesses? Yes, he acknowledged them himself. . . . His weaknesses were not concealed from the people. He was willing that people should know that he was mortal, and had failings. And so with President Young. Was not he a mortal man, a man who had weaknesses? He was not a God. He was not an immortal being. He was not infallible. No, he was fallible. And yet when he spoke by the power of God, it was the word of God to this people."[5]

Some members of the Church may ask why they are actually obligated to believe and follow the living prophet. And as strange as it may seem to others, it is a valid question. Sometimes we as a people tend to simply accept things as part of our culture without questioning where they came from or why they exist. In fact, if asked, some Latter-day Saints may not fully know why we are required to follow the living prophet.

The Lord gave the reason on the very day the Church was organized. In a revelation to the Church regarding His living prophet, the Lord declared:

> Wherefore, meaning the church, thou shalt give heed unto all his [the prophet's] words and commandments which he shall give unto you as he receiveth them, walking in all holiness before me;
>
> For his word ye shall receive, as if from mine own mouth, in all patience and faith.
>
> For by doing these things the gates of hell shall not prevail against you; yea, and the Lord God will disperse the powers of darkness from before you, and cause the heavens to shake for your good, and his name's glory. (D&C 21:4–6)

Simply put, those who wish to belong to the Church must receive the living prophet just as they would receive the Lord Himself. And although membership in the kingdom is voluntary, it requires adherence to all the "covenants, contracts, bonds, obligations, oaths, vows, performances, connections, associations, [and] expectations" (D&C 132:7) that the Lord has given or will ever give.

This covenant to believe and obey the living prophet when he speaks as the prophet has no limitations. The Lord made it clear in the above revelation: the Saints are to give heed unto all the prophet's words. And in this case, all means all, so long as the prophet speaks by virtue of his calling and not simply as a man stating his opinion.

Safety Following the Living Prophet

Some have difficulty believing and following the prophet without question or hesitation. They express concern that putting that much faith in one man is unnerving and could lead to egomania and tyranny. But this is the Lord's kingdom, and He has assured us that the prophet will never lead the Church astray. This also means that it is the *Lord's* place to set the Church in order, not ours. Since we did not call the prophet and set him apart and give him the keys of the kingdom, we have no authority as individuals to correct him or remove him from office. The living prophet is called by the Lord and answers to Him.

President Wilford Woodruff testified, "The Lord will never permit me or any other man who stands as President of this Church to lead you astray. It is not in the programme. It is not in the mind of God. If I were to attempt that, the Lord would remove me out of my place, and so He will any other man who attempts to lead the children of men astray from the oracles of God and from their duty."[6]

The Lord stated this same idea in a more dramatic way when He revealed to ancient Israel, "But the prophet, which shall presume to speak a word in my name, which I have not commanded him to speak . . . even that prophet shall die" (Deuteronomy 18:20).

We have nothing to fear by following the living prophet with all our hearts and minds.

Notes

1. Joseph Smith, *Teachings of the Prophet Joseph Smith,* sel. Joseph Fielding Smith (Salt Lake City: Deseret Book, 1976), 278.
2. Ibid., 268.
3. Ibid., 258.
4. Brigham Young, in *Journal of Discourses,* 26 vols. (London: Latter-day Saints' Book Depot, 1854–86), 13:95.
5. George Q. Cannon, in *Journal of Discourses,* 24:274.
6. Wilford Woodruff, 61st Semiannual General Conference of the Church, 6 October 1890; reported in *Deseret Evening News,* 11 October 1890, 2.

CHAPTER SIX

Principle 5: Other Church Leaders Are Authoritative Only When They Speak under the Direction of the Living Prophet

Although the living prophet is the only person on earth who can receive revelation and direction for the entire Church, the kingdom of God is one of participation, and thus, many others are called to assist in the work. In addition to local leadership at the ward and stake levels, the Lord has called and appointed General Authorities to assist the prophet in leading the Church throughout the world. Twelve of these men are set apart as members of the Quorum of the Twelve Apostles. These apostles have a sacred and holy calling.

The Lord declares that the Twelve Apostles are "called to declare my gospel, both unto Gentile and unto Jew" (D&C 18:26). They are "my disciples, and they shall take upon them my name . . . with full purpose of heart. . . . They are called to go into all the world to preach my gospel unto every creature" (D&C 18:27–28). They are "ordained of me to baptize in my name" and are "to declare my gospel, according to the power of the Holy Ghost" (D&C 18:29–32) "and to confirm those who are baptized into the church" (D&C 20:41). "It is the duty of the Twelve, also, to ordain and set in order all the other officers of the church" (D&C 107:58).

"The twelve traveling councilors are called to be the Twelve Apostles, or special witnesses of the name of Christ in all the world—thus differing from other officers in the church in the duties of their calling" (D&C 107:23). "The Twelve are a Traveling Presiding High Council, to officiate in the name of the Lord, *under the direction of the Presidency* of the Church, agreeable to the institution of heaven; to build up the church, and regulate all the affairs of the same in all nations" (D&C 107:33; emphasis added).

The Prophet Joseph Smith further described the calling and duties of the Twelve Apostles. In a meeting the prophet held with select Church leaders, he taught, "These are the Twelve Apostles, who are called to the office of the Traveling High Council, who are to preside over the churches of the Saints, among the Gentiles, where there is no presidency established; and they are to travel and preach among the Gentiles, until the Lord shall command them to go to the Jews. They are to hold the keys of this ministry, to unlock the door of the kingdom of heaven unto all nations, and to preach the gospel to every creature. This is the power, authority, and virtue of their apostleship."[1]

In another meeting with the Twelve, he explained that the authority of the Twelve "is next to the present Presidency . . . also the Twelve are not subject to any other than the First Presidency."[2] A few days later he "then called upon the quorums and congregation of Saints to acknowledge the Twelve Apostles, who were present, as prophets, seers, and revelators, and special witnesses to all the nations of the earth, holding the keys of the kingdom."[3] The calling of apostle is so special, in fact, the Lord declared personally that they are "mine apostles, even God's high priests; [and] are they whom my Father hath given me; ye are my friends" (D&C 84:63).

Another body of leaders in the Church is comprised of the Quorums of Seventy. The Lord revealed that "the Seventy are also called to preach the gospel, and to be especial witnesses unto the Gentiles and in all the world" (D&C 107:25). "The Seventy are to act in the name of the Lord, under the direction of the Twelve . . . in building up the church and regulating all the affairs of the same in all nations, first unto the Gentiles and then unto the Jews" (D&C 107:34).

The Seventy are called to assist the Twelve in their work of building up the kingdom, ministering to the various stakes and wards throughout the earth, and testifying of Christ and the restored gospel to those who are not of our faith. The office of Seventy was once a designation within the Melchizedek Priesthood organized at the ward level, but it now only exists at the highest levels of Church leadership and is organized into several quorums.

Together, the First Presidency, Quorum of the Twelve Apostles, and Quorums of Seventy comprise what are known as the General Authorities of the Church. Where various officers, such as bishops and stake presidents, have specific authority over their particular stewardships, General Authorities have just that—"general authority" over the entire Church.

However, even the Apostles and Seventies do not as individuals have keys to preside over or receive revelation for the entire Church. Only when they speak under the direction of the living prophet and their words are sanctioned by him is their counsel similarly binding. As the Lord revealed in section 43 of the Doctrine and Covenants, "But verily, verily, I say unto you, that *none else* [except the living prophet] shall be appointed unto this gift except it be through him" (D&C 43:4; emphasis added).

Some feel that because the members of the Quorum of Twelve Apostles are sustained as prophets, seers, and revelators they have the keys to receive revelation for the whole Church. But as the discussions of this subject in chapters 2 and 3 made clear, the living prophet is the only individual who has the right to receive revelation for the Church and authorize others to do so. Explaining the prophet's exclusive right to act on behalf of the Church, George Q. Cannon stated:

> There is but one man, (as you have often heard), at any given time on the earth, who holds this authority. There may be others who have this authority also; I thank God there are many who hold this authority—that is the authority of the Apostleship; but they hold it subordinate to the man who holds the keys, they cannot exercise this authority, only as he shall consent or delegate or authorize them to do so. There is but one man who has the power to exercise this authority, to stand, as it were, in God's stead, to be His voice unto the people, and that is the man who stands at the head and who is President, and who holds the keys by virtue of the appointment of God. God places him there. It is not man's act.[4]

It is true that the Apostles are ordained of the Lord and sustained by the Church membership as prophets, seers, and revelators. By virtue of this fact, they can and do receive revelation for and give direction to the general Church membership. However, the priesthood keys they hold to do this may only be exercised under the direction and with the permission of the living prophet who stands at the head of this Church on earth. President James E. Faust taught, "The greatest revelator in our time has been Joseph Smith. . . . Each of the 92 Apostles called since then has been sustained as a prophet, seer, and revelator. But the prophets, seers, and revelators succeeding Joseph as *Presidents of the Church* have been those Apostles in whom *all of the keys* of Christ's earthly kingdom have been active and functioning."[5]

This means that anything written, spoken, or done by a General Authority without being sanctioned by the living prophet does not constitute doctrine or commandment, and therefore, Church members are not under covenant to believe and obey. This includes books written by General Authorities that are not officially published by the Church, informal talks or addresses given by General Authorities, and personal opinions rendered by General Authorities formally or informally.

This does not mean that the words of General Authorities are of little value or that books written by them should not be purchased and treasured. The Brethren are knowledgeable, wise, and trustworthy men with spiritual insight and valuable life experience. Nevertheless, members of the Church should know exactly what they are under covenant to believe and obey and what they are not. We must be careful about what sources we turn to for "doctrine" when teaching lessons, giving talks, or explaining Church beliefs to members and nonmembers alike.

When I was a teenager, my hobbies included playing a particular game that I found fun, imaginative, and challenging. Shortly after I joined the Church, a well-intentioned member of my ward approached me and informed me that I should not be playing this particular game because it was condemned by the Church. When I asked him to clarify, he explained that the Brethren had declared this game inappropriate and forbade members from playing it.

As a fresh convert, I didn't know what to think. I knew the game in question had nothing to do with anything evil, and I had never heard anything about this from the missionaries who baptized me. I decided to look into the issue further. I discovered that the ward member had heard second (or third or fourth) hand that someone had said something about the game. I found that no General Authority said anything from the pulpit at general conference, nor had any authoritative declaration ever been issued by anyone. Even if a General Authority had made a statement about this game, I was under no obligation to observe it unless the living prophet sanctioned it in some way.

Hierarchy of Church Authority

To properly understand when the words and direction of other General Authorities are binding on the entire Church, we must first understand the hierarchical structure of Church leadership. When anyone asks me who the head of my Church is, I always respond, Jesus Christ. He is our Lord and our God and the founder of our Faith. Jesus Christ stands at the head of the Church that bears His name. The Apostle Paul explained that the Church is "built upon the foundation of the apostles and prophets, Jesus Christ himself being the chief corner stone" (Ephesians 2:20).

Christ has appointed a living prophet to lead and direct His work on the earth. This prophet, who is the president of the Church, is assisted by two counselors whom he chooses. As the Doctrine and Covenants states, "Wherefore, it must needs be that one be appointed of the High Priesthood to preside over the priesthood, and he shall be called President of the High Priesthood of the Church" (D&C 107:65). "Of the Melchizedek Priesthood, three Presiding High Priests . . . form a quorum of the Presidency of the Church" (D&C 107:22).

The president of the Church is the only person who has authority to exercise all of the keys of the kingdom and who has the sole right to preside over the Church, but the First Presidency is the ultimate quorum with the right to preside over the Church.

Next to the First Presidency, the Twelve Apostles hold the keys to govern and lead the Church. According to revelation, "The twelve traveling councilors are called to be the Twelve Apostles. . . . And they form a quorum, equal in authority and power to the three presidents previously mentioned" (D&C 107:23–24).

After the Quorum of the Twelve, "the Seventy are also called to preach the gospel, and to be especial witnesses unto the Gentiles and in all the world. . . . And they form a quorum, equal in authority to that of the Twelve special witnesses or Apostles just named" (D&C 107:25–26).

These revelations identify the three quorums that preside over the whole Church. But although these passages identify them as equal to one another in authority, keys, and power, it is important to understand that they are not all equal at the same time. The First Presidency has ultimate authority to preside over the Church and has authority over the Twelve Apostles and the Quorum of the Seventy. As the Prophet Joseph Smith taught, the Twelve "are not subject to any other than the First Presidency, viz., Sidney Rigdon, and Frederick G. Williams, who are now my Counselors, and where I am not, there is no First Presidency over the Twelve."[6]

President Joseph F. Smith, desired to correct the "impression" among some Church members that the "Twelve Apostles possess equal authority with the First Presidency in the Church." In doing so he stated that although the doctrine "is correct when there is no other Presidency but the Twelve Apostles" as long as there are "three presiding elders who possess the presiding authority in the Church, the authority of the Twelve Apostles is not equal to theirs." Therefore, he concluded, "So long as there is a First Presidency in the Church they hold supreme authority in the Church, and the Twelve Apostles are subject unto them and do not possess the same authority as they do as a presiding quorum."[7]

Expanding this same theme, President Joseph F. Smith pointed out that some people "have thought also that the quorum of the seventies possess equal authority with that of the First Presidency and with the Twelve. So they would if there was no Presidency and no Twelve and only seven elders called seventies in the Church, but their authority is not equal to that of the First Presidency while the First Presidency lives, nor to that of the Twelve Apostles."[8]

The First Presidency presides over the Church and over all quorums in it until the death of the president of the Church. When this occurs, the First Presidency dissolves, and the right to preside over the Church falls on the Quorum of the Twelve. President Joseph F. Smith again taught, "When the Lord takes away the man who is called to be the president of the Church and the quorum of the three Presidents is thereby dissolved, then the authority of the Twelve rises to the dignity of the Presidents of the Church and not till then."[9]

Because the keys of the Church that are held by the Twelve Apostles become active upon the dissolution of the First Presidency, the Twelve have the right to appoint a new president of the Church by revelation. Traditionally, this has always been the Apostle with the most seniority, the President of the Quorum of the Twelve. President Wilford Woodruff taught that the President of the Twelve "is really the President of the Church by virtue of his office as much while presiding over the Twelve Apostles as over his two counselors."[10] So, upon the death of a Church President, the President of the Twelve becomes the Lord's living prophet to whom we must look and whom we must sustain.[11]

But what if the Twelve Apostles could not preside over the Church upon the death of the president of the Church? Because the revelation clearly states that the Seventy have the same authority as the Twelve, the right to preside would fall upon this next quorum. President Joseph F. Smith again explained that if the First Presidency "were to be killed off, then the Council of the Twelve Apostles would stand in their place and preside until the Presidency should be restored; and if they and the First Presidency were all killed off, then the seventies would come forward and they would establish the order of Zion and renew the order of the priesthood upon the earth."[12]

What a beautiful way the Lord has provided for His Church and kingdom to be led and sustained without interruption or confusion through a hierarchy of General Authorities and priesthood leaders.

Words of the Twelve and Seventy Binding upon the Church

Although the living prophet is the only individual on earth at a given time who is authorized to receive revelation, give commandment, and set doctrine for the Church, the Apostles and Seventies are also authorized to do these things under the direction of the living prophet. In other words, when the living prophet has specifically authorized these other men to speak officially for the Church or has sanctioned their words and actions after the fact, their directives and commandments are binding upon all the Saints.

Instances when the words of General Authorities are universally binding include talks at general conference, articles in Church publications like the *Ensign*, or when they teach Church doctrine established by the president of the Church, current or past. Other instances would include a situation where the living prophet dies and the Twelve are leading the Church, or if the Seventy ever had custodial authority over the kingdom.

The validity of the General Authorities' teachings and commandments to the Saints follows the same pattern given by the Lord to another General Authority, Oliver Cowdery. Section 28 of the Doctrine and Covenants reveals:

> And if thou [Oliver] art led at any time by the Comforter to speak or teach, or at all times by the way of commandment unto the church, thou mayest do it. But thou shalt not write by way of commandment, but by wisdom; and thou shalt not command him who is at thy head, and at the head of the church; for I have given him the keys of the

> mysteries, and the revelations which are sealed, until I shall appoint unto them another in his stead. . . . and thou shalt have revelations, but write them not by way of commandment. (D&C 28:4–8)

As with the above direction to Oliver Cowdery, members of the Twelve and the Seventy may not of themselves establish commandment or revelation for the Church and may not command the living prophet. The Lord promises the other General Authorities revelation, but Church members should not consider them commandments unless delivered or authorized by the living prophet. Again, this is not to say that they are false or worthless. Rather, it means that Church members are not bound by covenant to accept and obey them unless specifically sanctioned by the living prophet.

Notes

1. Joseph Smith, *Teachings of the Prophet Joseph Smith,* sel. Joseph Fielding Smith (Salt Lake City: Deseret Book, 1976), 74.
2. Ibid., 105–6.
3. Ibid., 109.
4. George Q. Cannon, in *Journal of Discourses,* 26 vols. (London: Latter-day Saints' Book Depot, 1854–86), 24:274–75.
5. James E. Faust, "Continuing Revelation," *Ensign,* August, 1996, 2; emphasis added.
6. Smith, *Teachings,* 106.
7. Joseph F. Smith, in *Elders' Journal of The Church of Jesus Christ of Latter-day Saints* (Far West, Missouri: Thomas B. Marsh, 1838), 4:43.
8. Ibid.
9. Ibid.
10. *Wilford Woodruff, His Life and Labours,* comp. Matthias F. Cowley (Salt Lake City: Deseret News, 1916), 561.
11. The tradition of the president of the Twelve becoming the next president of the Church was established by the Lord through Joseph Smith and has continued to this day. If it were ever to change, it would be at the Lord's discretion and would be done through a unanimous vote by the Quorum of the Twelve Apostles.
12. Joseph F. Smith, in *Elders' Journal,* 4:45–46.

CHAPTER SEVEN

Principle 6: The Living Prophet's Words Are Preeminent Over Past Prophets

Because The Church of Jesus Christ of Latter-day Saints is a living Church, it requires living, continuing revelation and direction from God. Without this current and up-to-date guidance and instruction, the Church would eventually become what all other churches are—man-made organizations that rely only on past traditions for present and future direction. Because of this, these churches have become dead—not in terms of the goodness of many of their members, but in the life-giving authority and power of heaven needed to be spiritually alive and vital. As the Prophet Joseph Smith taught, "The sectarian priests are blind, and they lead the blind, and they will all fall into the ditch together. They build with hay, wood, and stubble, on the old revelations, without the true priesthood or spirit of revelation."[1]

But the Lord insures that His Church has access to priesthood authority and to living spiritual power. He has established a system whereby His kingdom on earth will always have a living prophet to lead and guide His people. The most important part of this leadership role is the ability to continue to receive living, current revelation from God.

The Church needs continuing, up-to-date revelation and direction, as God's people in all ages have, to deal with issues that pertain specifically to our day and our particular circumstances. For example, although the Ten Commandments remain valuable and pertinent to us today, the commandment to gather manna or abstain from pork does not apply as it did when Israel wandered in the wilderness.

Speaking of the necessity of continuing revelation, President John Taylor testified that the Church needs "a living tree—a living fountain—living intelligence, proceeding from the living priesthood in heaven, through the living priesthood on earth. . . . And from the time that Adam first received a communication from God, to the time that John, on the Isle of Patmos, received his communication, or Joseph Smith had the heavens opened to him, it always required new revelations, adapted to the peculiar circumstances in which the churches or individuals were placed."

President Taylor pointed out that "Adam's revelation did not instruct Noah to build his ark; nor did Noah's revelation tell Lot to forsake Sodom; nor did either of these speak of the departure of the children of Israel from Egypt. These all had revelations for themselves, and so had Isaiah, Jeremiah, Ezekiel, Jesus, Peter, Paul, John, and Joseph. And so must we, or we shall make a shipwreck."[2]

In addition to receiving living revelation to meet current circumstances, we need a living prophet for another important reason. The purpose of the gospel is to bring us back into God's presence (whether this occurs before or after we die), and the Lord has sent prophets into the world to teach us how to return. However, returning to the presence of the Lord is a process—of faith, sacrifice, knowledge, struggle, and discovery. We grow "line upon line, precept upon precept; here a little, and there a little" (D&C 128:21) making major strides forward at various pivotal points in our lives.

And as we change and grow closer to Christ and develop a greater spiritual depth, we need a guide at each one of these pivotal points along the way. We can't rely solely on the teachings of past prophets for our personal direction. We need a living guide who can minister to us and show us in a personal way each step on our path to perfection. This is the role of the living prophet—in connection, of course, with the teachings of past prophets, the holy scriptures, and the personal revelation we receive from the Holy Ghost.

The Living Prophet Can Supersede Past Teachings

More than simply receiving revelation to deal with current circumstances, the living prophet's role is so significant that he even has authority to amend or seemingly contradict statements of his predecessors. This is vital to understand. Saints in all ages have fallen into apostasy when they chose to cling to the teachings of long-dead prophets while rejecting the living prophet. Claiming integrity by holding fast to what *has* been given, they refuse to receive what yet needs to be given. They suppose past prophets had a greater ability to receive the Lord's word to His people than the living revelator. Ironically, those who reject the Lord's current prophet usually cite the teachings of past authorities to justify their position, when the living prophet himself has the sole right to interpret these past authorities for the Church. Sadly, those who set themselves up in opposition to the living oracle and do not repent, have and always will find themselves eventually out of the kingdom.

Explaining the preeminence of a living revelator, President George Q. Cannon stated:

> If the prophets of God of old wrote and spoke as they were moved upon by the Holy Ghost, there are prophets of God living upon the earth today who can speak and write as they are moved upon by the same power. And the word of God that comes down from heaven in our day is just as authoritative as the word of God that came in times of old . . . it is of *much more importance* to the people called Latter-day Saints, because it comes direct to them from our living head.[3]

Reaffirming this principle, President Ezra Taft Benson testified, "The most important prophet, so far as we are concerned, is the one who is living in our day and age. This is the prophet who has instructions from God to us today. God's revelation to Adam did not instruct Noah to build the ark. Every generation has need of the ancient scripture plus the current scripture from the living prophet. Therefore," he concluded, "the most crucial reading and pondering which you should do is of the latest inspired words from the Lord's mouthpiece."[4]

Some members of the Church take offense at the idea that the living prophet has the right to change a principle or practice established by a past prophet. But history is replete with instances in which prophets have done exactly this. For example, the law of Moses replaced the higher law established by Adam and the other ancient patriarchs, Christ did away with animal sacrifice after His atonement, and the Sabbath day was changed from Saturday to Sunday to commemorate Christ's resurrection. Although the early disciples were to preach the gospel exclusively to the Jews, Peter soon received a revelation commanding him to take the gospel to the Gentiles. Circumcision was a requirement for anyone wishing to become a member of the house of Israel, but the practice soon became optional for those belonging to the New Testament Church.

Even in the early days of this dispensation, commandments, practices, and policies were altered, amended, and modified to meet existing circumstances or to otherwise satisfy the Lord's will. For example, because the Saints in Missouri were not able to fully live the law of consecration, this economic program was placed on hold, and the Saints were eventually left with the law of tithing only. The office of Seventy at the ward level was eliminated, all worthy males were allowed to hold the priesthood after 1978, and the temple ceremony has been refined several times over the past 150 years.

Were all these changes and seeming contradictions wrong, or did they somehow violate previous commandments? The answer, of course, is *no.* The Lord fully understands what He does and why He does it. Man's weakness and lack of understanding does not constitute a mistake on God's part or on the part of His living prophet. Since it is God's right to give commandment and establish practice and policy, it is His right alone to change it any time He sees fit. As the Lord stated in the Doctrine and Covenants, "Wherefore I, the Lord, command and revoke, as it seemeth me good" (D&C 56:4).

One of the major changes that took place in the Church in this dispensation was the elimination of the practice of plural marriage. Those who either left the Church over it or were excommunicated because they refused to abandon the practice argued that President Wilford Woodruff was uninspired. They based their accusation on the grounds that plural marriage was a law of God instituted by the Prophet Joseph Smith. However, these apostates failed to realize that the institution of plural marriage itself seemingly contradicted several long-established scriptural commandments.

For example, the Old Testament states, "Neither shall he multiply wives to himself, that his heart turn not away" (Deuteronomy 17:17), while Paul taught that a bishop should be "the husband of one wife"

(1 Timothy 3:2). Condemning many of the Nephites, Jacob commanded that "there shall not any man among you have save it be one wife; and concubines he shall have none" (Jacob 2:27). The Lord commanded in the Doctrine and Covenants that the brethren "shalt love thy wife with all thy heart, and shalt cleave unto her and none else" (D&C 42:22) because "it is lawful that he should have one wife, and they twain shall be one flesh" (D&C 49:16). Of course, the commandment given by the Prophet to practice plural marriage in no way contradicted these scriptures or violated previous commandments. But the same logic employed by apostates against President Wilford Woodruff's Manifesto only succeeded in destroying their claim to plural marriage.

We need to realize that commandments and rules are not the ultimate purpose of our worship. Instead, they are given as a means of helping us learn obedience and faith in order to become like our Heavenly Father. In other words, the commandments exist for us, not the other way around. Christ explained this principle to the Pharisees (who, by the way, were fanatics about rules and regulations). He taught them, "The sabbath was made for man, and not man for the sabbath. Therefore the Son of man is Lord also of the sabbath" (Mark 2:27–28).

As the Prophet Joseph Smith explained, "That which is wrong under one circumstance, may be, and often is, right under another. God said, 'Thou shalt not kill'; at another time He said, 'Thou shalt utterly destroy.' This is the principle on which the government of heaven is conducted—by revelation adapted to the circumstances in which the children of the kingdom are placed. Whatever God requires is right, no matter what it is, although we may not see the reason thereof till long after the events transpire."[5]

God the Same Yesterday, Today, and Forever

When I first joined the Church, I discovered the scripture that said "God is the same yesterday, today, and forever" (Mormon 9:9). I loved this maxim at first, but I soon became discouraged. As I studied the scriptures and especially Church history, I began to see how many commandments and practices had changed over the years. I did not have much of an issue with the Lord changing things according to His will, but I could not reconcile how He could do this and still maintain that He was the same "yesterday, today, and forever."

Thankfully, I had good teachers and friends to rely on, and I soon learned the fundamental difference between "eternal, unchanging truth" and "policies and practices." God has never, nor will ever, alter or compromise eternal truth. This is the basis of His power, of all that He is. He will never violate agency, for example, nor will He ever break a law that He has agreed to follow. On the other hand, He gives commandments to His children for their benefit, and He alters or amends them for their greater good and happiness. God is therefore the same yesterday, today, and forever for two reasons: 1) He never violates eternal, unchanging truth; 2) He changes commandments and practices because His work is constant and unchanging—"to bring to pass the immortality and eternal life of man" (Moses 1:39).

Living Prophet More Important Than the Scriptures

What Is Scripture?

Most people assume the word "scripture" refers to the standard works of the Church. Although this is the best known and most recognizable kind of scripture, it does not accurately define what scripture is. According to the Bible Dictionary, anything "which is spoken under the influence of the Holy Ghost" is scripture. But not all scripture is exactly the same or equally authoritative.

There are three types of scripture. The first and most basic type can be referred to as "personal scripture." This is received by individuals through the Holy Ghost and is given in various ways, including dreams, visions, visitations, inspiration, audible instruction, and so on. So long as it comes from a divine source it can be considered scripture. However, personal scripture is exactly that—personal. It is given for the benefit of the individual who received it. It is in no way binding on the general Church membership or on any other person.

The second type of scripture is that which is given to the Saints through various priesthood leaders. For example, when a bishop gets divine direction for his ward and reveals it by the keys of his office, the ward members are to consider it scripture. When a mission president receives divine direction for his stewardship and tells his missionaries, they need to consider it scripture. Or when a member of the Quorums of the Seventy visits a stake conference and gives specific instruction, the members of that stake must consider it scripture. The Lord revealed in relation to Church priesthood leaders, "And whatsoever they shall speak when moved upon by the Holy Ghost shall be scripture, shall be the will of the Lord, shall be the mind of the Lord, shall be the word of the Lord, shall be the voice of the Lord, and the power of God unto salvation" (D&C 68:4).

As discussed in chapter 2, revelation given through a particular priesthood leader is only binding on those over whom the leader has stewardship, not on the entire Church. Therefore, what is revealed by a leader (other than the living prophet) does not constitute scripture for the Church, only for those over whom the leader has stewardship.

The third and most important type of scripture is that which comes through the living prophet. This includes any revelation, commandment, proclamation, policy, or instruction given to the Church, any of its members, or those who do not believe in the gospel. It is binding on those to whom it is directed, and they are obligated to believe and obey. As the Lord revealed on the day the Church was organized, "Thou shalt give heed unto all his [the prophet's] words and commandments which he shall give unto you as he receiveth them, walking in all holiness before me; for his word ye shall receive as if from mine own mouth" (D&C 21:4–5).

This type of scripture originated with Adam. When he first taught his children the mysteries of heaven and gave them commandments that would return them to the presence of God, he recorded his words and kept a "book of remembrance" (Moses 6:5) for future generations. As subsequent prophets preached the word of God, they too recorded their teachings and commandments, adding them to the writings of those who came before. This is how "the scriptures" came to be and were made available to mankind.

And although we do not currently have the complete writings of all the prophets, the pattern for receiving and recording scripture has remained consistent to the present day. First, the Lord speaks to His prophets and reveals a portion of His truth. The prophets then proclaim that truth, and the revelation is recorded. It matters little whether the Lord initiates the revelation or simply responds to a query from His servants. After all, He anticipates the need for it long before His children ever think about it.

This third type of scripture can be divided into two categories: canonized scripture and all other kinds. Canonized scripture is that which is presented to and sustained by the general Church membership as the authorized word of the Lord to the Church and the world. This does not mean that other teachings and publications are not authoritative or binding, they are just not officially presented to the general membership of the Church for specific sustaining. The current Canon of the Church consists of the Holy Bible, the Book of Mormon, the Doctrine and Covenants, and the Pearl of Great Price. These four books comprise what are referred to as the standard works.

The second category of scripture that comes through the living prophet consists of everything received under the priesthood keys he holds. This includes official proclamations and declarations, periodic letters of instruction to stake and ward membership, Church publications, addresses, interviews, and the list goes on. This scripture is as equally binding on the Church and the world as canonized scripture is, without having to be presented and officially sustained each time by the general Church membership.

The Importance of Scripture

The scriptures are of great worth and importance to all those who wish to follow God and be saved in the kingdom of heaven. The standard works, especially, hold tremendous value and are to be treasured by each and every member of the Church. The Prophet Joseph Smith taught that the scriptures are "given by direct inspiration for the good of man. We believe that God condescended to speak from the heavens and declare His will concerning the human family, to give them just and holy laws, to regulate their conduct, and guide them in a direct way, that in due time He might take them to Himself and make them joint heirs with His Son."[6] The Lord testified, "And the Book of Mormon and the holy scriptures are given of me for your instruction; and the power of my Spirit quickeneth all things" (D&C 33:16).

Scripture and the Living Prophet

As valuable as they are, the standard works are not the most important source of God's word to us in our day. Because the living prophet's position is preeminent over past prophets, his word is more authoritative and of more worth to us in our day than even the holy scriptures. As such, he has authority to amend or contradict anything found in scripture—including the standard works. President John Taylor testified, "Those books are good for example, precedent, and investigation, and for developing certain laws and principles; but they do not, they cannot touch every case required to be adjudicated and set in order."[7]

The doctrine that the living prophet's words are preeminent over written, canonized scripture was perhaps never more dramatically illustrated than by the Prophet Joseph Smith and President Brigham Young. During the Kirtland period, Joseph often held or attended meetings for his family, close friends, and a few visitors to discuss the gospel and share testimonies and insights with one another. During one such meeting, a person described as a "leading man in the Church" arose at the invitation of the prophet and began a discourse on the sacred character of the holy scriptures. His address was eloquent and powerful and his commitment to the scriptures commendable, but he soon began moving into dangerous territory.

He boldly testified that the scriptures were so true, anyone who taught a principle or doctrine that contradicted them was out of harmony with the gospel. He went on to vehemently claim that modern prophets were confined by what was stated in scripture, and that if they taught any more or less than the letter of scripture, they were overstepping their authority as the Lord's representatives.

As patient and loving as the Prophet was, he allowed the man to finish his remarks and thanked him for his preparation and contribution. He then turned to Brigham Young and said, "Brother Brigham, I would like you to take the stand and tell us your views with regard to the living oracles and the written word of God."

Brigham immediately jumped to his feet. He laid down the standard works one by one in front of everybody, then boldly and plainly testified, "There is the written word of God to us, concerning the work of God from the beginning of the world, almost to our day. And now, when compared to the living oracles those books are nothing to me; those books do not convey the word of God direct to us now, as do the words of a prophet or a man bearing the Holy Priesthood in our day and generation. I would rather have the living oracles than all the writing in the books."

With the power of the Spirit, Brigham Young taught a fundamental restored principle while at the same time correcting the misguided brother who had just spoken. He declared that the scriptures, although valuable, were nothing next to the word of the Lord's living prophet. He explained that the written word was little better than dead letters without a living prophet to interpret and explain them. So bold and powerful was Brigham as he spoke by the Spirit—under the direction and at the discretion of the prophet—that all in the room were converted to the truth of his words. Even the misguided brother was converted. But to put the Lord's official seal of approval on the teaching, the Prophet Joseph Smith stood after Brigham had finished and stated, "Brother Brigham has told you the word of the Lord, and he has told you the truth."[8]

Affirming this principle, Orson Pratt taught, "The very moment that we set aside the living oracles we set aside the revelations of God. Why? Because the revelations of God command us plainly that we shall hearken to the living oracles. Hence, if we undertake to follow the written word, and at the same time do not give heed to the living oracles of God, the written word will condemn us."[9]

Adding his testimony of the same truth, President George Q. Cannon testified that all the standard works of the Church, "without the living oracles and a constant stream of revelation from the Lord, would not lead any people into the celestial kingdom. . . . This may seem a strange declaration to make, but strange as it may sound, it is nevertheless true." President Cannon held the standard works sacred and of infinite value, but "in and of themselves, with all the light that they give, they are insufficient to guide the children of men and to lead them into the presence of God." To be led this way, he asserted, "requires a living priesthood and constant revelation from God to the people according to the circumstances in which they may be placed."[10]

Past Prophets and the Living Prophet

It seems curious that anyone would accept the teachings and commandments of past prophets while rejecting some or all of the words of the living prophet. As President Spencer W. Kimball once expressed, "Many are prone to garnish the sepulchers of yesterday's prophets and mentally stone the living ones."[11] Nevertheless, this has happened far too often in the Church and continues to occur. Perhaps discovering why this happens may help us avoid the pitfall.

There are at least three reasons why people cling to past prophets and reject the living prophet. First, with human nature as it is, people can be prone to find fault with the living prophet because (1) he is imperfect, and (2) he is alive to prove it. By contrast, it is much more difficult to find fault with past prophets because they aren't around to expose their weaknesses and mistakes.

Of course, this does not mean they were any less susceptible to imperfections than the current living prophet; but for some reason many people prefer to think of those who have passed on in the most favorable light. And although thinking idealistically about the deceased is a good thing, the living deserve the same consideration—especially the living prophet.

The second reason some cling inappropriately to past prophets is that these men are not around to rebuke or condemn when their words are not heeded. Whenever a prophet is given commandment or instruction by the Lord to proclaim, he is under obligation to do all he can to insure that it is understood and obeyed. If not, the prophet has the right to call the people to repentance. As the Prophet Joseph Smith explained:

> One great privilege of the priesthood is to obtain revelations of the mind and will of God. It is also the privilege of the Melchizedek Priesthood, to reprove, rebuke, and admonish, as well as to receive revelation. . . . I frequently rebuke and admonish my brethren, and that because I love them, not because I wish to incur their displeasure or mar their happiness. Such a course of conduct is not calculated to gain the good will of all, but rather the ill will of many . . . but these rebukes and admonitions become necessary.[12]

Mormon taught that these rebukes and admonitions are necessary because, "Except the Lord doth chasten his people . . . they will not remember him" (Helaman 12:3). Sadly, however, the Lord's prophet almost always encounters those who refuse to follow him and take offense because of his reproof. As Nephi put it, "The guilty taketh the truth to be hard, for it cutteth them to the very center" (1 Nephi 16:2).

When a particular prophet is not alive to rebuke or condemn, he can be remembered more fondly. However, when the living prophet is personally involved in our lives, his call to repentance stands as an ever-present reminder to the wicked that they cannot be lulled "away into carnal security" believing that "all is well in Zion" (2 Nephi 28:21).

The third reason people look to past prophets and reject the living prophet goes hand in hand with the second. It is easier to follow the words of past prophets because they have spoken what they have spoken, and will give no more. This makes it easy to deal with them because people know what to expect; there are no surprises. These past prophets will not be giving any new doctrines or commandments.

By contrast, the living prophet never finishes his work until he dies. Because of this, no one knows (including him) what new direction or commandments he could receive at any time. He may even receive something that contradicts what he himself established previously. Such a possibility is extremely unsettling to the prideful. For some reason, they fear change and need to feel they will not be caught off guard at any time. Of course, the Lord's purpose in revealing new directives and commandments is not to toy with His children. But those who allow themselves to be so vexed by change need to learn that the Lord requires His Saints to "be thou humble; and the Lord thy God shall lead thee by the hand" (D&C 112:10), "[for] I will lead them withersoever I will, and no power shall stay my hand" (D&C 38:33).

Rejecting the Living Prophet for Dead Ones

Clinging to past prophets in order to justify rejecting the living prophet brings painful results. A person will lose the Spirit, lose his testimony, and eventually, if he does not repent, lose Church membership. I know a man who fell into the trap of clinging so rigidly to past prophets that he lost everything he once held dear.

The situation began years ago when he allowed himself to become frustrated with the way Church leaders handled a particular matter that he considered extremely important. And although the issue was important, this brother became progressively more upset with the Brethren. He sighted past Church presidents and other leaders to defend his position and attempted to prove the current administration was somehow "out of harmony." He assumed that because the General Authorities did not see things the way he did, and failed to do what he would have were he in charge, they must have been wrong and unfit to lead—at least in this matter.

The problem with his assumption, however, was that he was not leading the Church. He was not called to any position of authority to speak on behalf of the Lord, and he held no keys to administer the kingdom of God on earth. As such, he was not authorized to interpret the teachings or programs of past Church Presidents.

Claiming an unwavering faith, he held steadfastly to less-important principles established by past prophets and abandoned the indispensable principle of sustaining the Lord's living prophet. This brother became so obsessed with his crusade that he began to vilify the prophet and other General Authorities. He became consumed with anger and criticism and stopped coming to Church. He eventually lost his testimony and everything else in his life that used to matter to him. His wife sued for divorce, his business dwindled, his standing in the community was ruined because of his emotional and spiritual instability, and he was eventually excommunicated. Even his friends who were faithful members of the Church were forced to avoid him because he sought to lead them down the same road he had gone.

This story is indeed a tragic one. And perhaps the most tragic thing of all is that this man became so consumed by his zeal, he failed to clearly see the great irony in all of it. He originally became critical of the General Authorities because he did not believe they were being true to an important aspect of the gospel, as taught by past prophets. However, through his apostasy he lost everything that past prophets have taught to be most important—Church membership, priesthood, temple marriage and family, happiness, humility, success, and peace. What a remarkable example of how clinging to past prophets in defiance of the living prophet only destroys all that the past prophets stand for.

Notes

1. Joseph Smith, *Teachings of the Prophet Joseph Smith,* sel. Joseph Fielding Smith (Salt Lake City: Deseret Book, 1976), 311.
2. John Taylor, in *Millennial Star,* 1 November, 1847, 323.
3. George Q. Cannon, in *Journal of Discourses,* 26 vols. (London: Latter-day Saints' Book Depot, 1854–86), 24:85; emphasis added.
4. Ezra Taft Benson, "Jesus Christ—Gifts and Expectations," *New Era,* May 1975, 16.
5. Smith, *Teachings,* 256.
6. Ibid., 53–54.
7. Taylor, in *Millennial Star,* 1 November, 1847, 323.
8. Wilford Woodruff, in Conference Reports of The Church of Jesus Christ of Latter-day Saints (Salt Lake City: The Church of Jesus Christ of Latter-day Saints, 1898 to present), October 1897, 18–19.
9. Orson Pratt, in *Journal of Discourses,* 7:373.
10. George Q. Cannon, *Gospel Truth: Discourses and Writings of President George Q. Cannon,* ed. Jerreld L. Newquist (Salt Lake City: Deseret Book, 1974), 252.
11. Spencer W. Kimball, *Instructor,* 95:257.
12. Smith, *Teachings,* 111–13.

CHAPTER EIGHT

Principle 7: If the Living Prophet Has Not Contradicted Past Teachings, They Are Still in Full Force

Chapter 7 established the principle that the living prophet has the right and authority to amend or supersede the teachings and doctrines of past prophets. But does this mean that when a new prophet is sustained, all previous teachings, commandments, and doctrines suddenly become invalid? Obviously, such a thing would be absurd. After the Twelve and the body of the Church had sustained Brigham Young as the next prophet, basic Church doctrines taught by the Prophet Joseph Smith were not suddenly discarded. When Joseph F. Smith became president of the Church following Lorenzo Snow's death, the Saints continued to pay tithing. When Ezra Taft Benson succeeded Spencer W. Kimball, certain Church members were not stripped of the priesthood based on their race.

It makes sense then, that what has been established in the past by any of the prophets must be considered by the Church to be doctrine and commandment unless or until the living prophet changes it. Said another way, where the living prophet has not officially taught a principle that revises the position of a previous prophet, the former teaching remains in effect, and we are just as obligated to believe and obey as if the living prophet had established it himself.

Reinforcing the principle that previous doctrines remain in force unless amended or changed by the living prophet, the Prophet Joseph Smith once taught: "We never inquire at the hand of God for special revelation only in case of their being no previous revelation to suit the case."[1]

In this passage the Prophet revealed the principle that there is no need to receive special revelation on a matter if it has already been given—whether by a previous Church president or by an ancient prophet whose commandments have been established in the standard works.

Shortly after the death of one of the Church presidents, I overheard several members of a neighboring stake discussing the change in leadership. One brother who was a veteran of the stake remarked, "I am glad we have a new prophet; he sure is more in line with what this Church should be doing. I didn't much care for the old one; he kept teaching things I just couldn't swallow. Now that he's gone, we'll finally get things right again."

In addition to lacking the necessary respect for priesthood authority, this brother clearly misunderstood how the kingdom of God operates. He assumed that everything in the Church would suddenly change because a new President was sustained. It is true that each Church president has a particular emphasis—President Lorenzo Snow had tithing, President David O. McKay had member missionary work, President Benson had the Book of Mormon, and President Gordon B. Hinckley began a massive temple-building effort. But all of the living prophets of this dispensation have preached the same gospel, taught the same doctrine, and, with needed exceptions, continued those programs established by their predecessors. The sustaining of a new prophet has never meant the complete dismissal of that which came before.

The closest the world has ever come to a "brand new gospel" program occurred in the meridian of time during Jesus' earthly ministry. He taught the Nephites, "Therefore those things which were of old time, which were under the law [of Moses], in me are all fulfilled. Old things are done away, and all things have become new" (3 Nephi 12:46–47).

However, He later clarified this statement by teaching:

> Marvel not that I said unto you that old things had passed away, and that all things had become new. Behold, I say unto you that the law is fulfilled that was given unto Moses. . . . Behold, I do not destroy

> the prophets, for as many as have not been fulfilled in me . . . shall all be fulfilled. And because I said unto you that old things have passed away, I do not destroy that which hath been spoken concerning things which are to come. For behold, the covenant which I have made with my people is not all fulfilled; but the law which was given unto Moses hath an end in me. (3 Nephi 15:3–4, 6–8)

Even when Christ came to put old things away and establish a new covenant, He referred to the law of Moses, which He gave to the children of Israel because they rejected the original gospel preached by Adam, Enoch, Noah, Abraham, and Moses.

Although the Savior fulfilled the law of Moses and did away with many of its practices, most of the core commandments remained. For example, all of the Ten Commandments remain in full force to this day. Murder is still a sin, as is adultery, theft, idol worship, and lying. The Sabbath day is still holy and needs to be observed, and children are still required to honor their parents. Practices like animal sacrifice and circumcision are no longer required, but most of the core commandments remain a part of the gospel covenant Christ reestablished both in the meridian of time and in these latter days.

In most cases, to sustain the living prophet requires us to sustain past prophets. Although the living prophet's words are preeminent over those who have come before, he rests on a foundation of doctrine, policy, commandment, and teachings established by his predecessors. When President Joseph F. Smith held the position of president of the Church and living prophet, he acknowledged the validity and authority of those who preceded him. He declared:

> I bear testimony to you and to the world, that Joseph Smith was raised up by the power of God to lay the foundation of this great latter-day work, to reveal the fulness of the gospel to the world in this dispensation, to restore the Priesthood of God to the world . . .
>
> I bear testimony to the divine authority of those who succeeded the Prophet Joseph Smith in the presidency of this Church. They were men of God. I knew them; I was intimately associated with them . . . so I can bear testimony to the integrity, to the honor, to the purity of life, to the intelligence, and to the divinity of the mission and calling of Brigham Young, of John, of Wilford, and of Lorenzo. They were inspired of God to fill the mission to which they were called . . . I thank God for that testimony and for the Spirit that *prompts me and impels me towards these men, toward their mission* . . . and I pray earnestly that it may never depart from me.[7]

Even as the one man on earth preeminent over his predecessors, President Joseph F. Smith acknowledged his and the Church's dependence on the doctrines, teachings, and policies established by past prophets.

However, some members balk at the opportunity of taking advantage of the heritage left by past prophets. For example, I attended a meeting several years ago conducted by a missionary couple who were putting on workshops for the various zones in the mission. The subject of these workshops focused on how to deal with investigators' concerns about what some would call "deep doctrines." The couple distributed a quiz with several true/false questions relating to some of the more common doctrines in question. When the missionaries had completed the quiz, the couple reviewed it, explaining that it was a trick, and each one of the questions should have been answered "false." Several of the missionaries objected to the couple's dismissal of certain teachings, arguing that although they do not necessarily belong in the missionary discussions, they were most certainly true.

When the couple asked the elders and sisters to defend their assumptions, they cited several of the earlier leaders of the Church, including Joseph Smith, Brigham Young, John Taylor, Heber C. Kimball, and Orson Pratt. The response of the older missionary couple was astounding. They told the zone, "Oh you can't really rely on those early Brethren; they tended to get a lot of things mixed up." A reference was even made to Brigham Young and his "habit for preaching false doctrine."

While the purpose of this chapter is not to personally attack anyone or to stir up controversy about particular doctrines taught by the early Church leaders, it is important to clear up some harmful misconceptions. First, the early prophets and apostles of this dispensation were great men who had magnificent spiritual insight and knowledge. They were personally visited and instructed by heavenly messengers ranging from the Savior to ancient patriarchs like Adam, Moses, Elijah, Peter, and others.

Second, Joseph Smith, Brigham Young, John Taylor, and others were living prophets and presidents of the Church. What they taught the Saints by the keys of that position constituted the word of the Lord in their day—sacred and binding. Their words are equally binding on us today unless the living prophet amends them. And only the living prophet is authorized to do so. It will not do for individual members of the Church to decide for themselves the limitations of a prophet's calling, whether he is alive or dead. Doing so puts them in a position that God has not called them to.

Dismissing Past Prophets

Why are some people tempted to dismiss the teachings of past prophets after a new prophet takes over? It would seem that this occurs for the same reason that some dismiss the living prophet and cling to past ones: they want to justify their beliefs, opinions, and actions that are out of harmony with the current program. If they disagree with or are threatened by a teaching or commandment of the living prophet, they conveniently find reason to criticize and attack him. Likewise, if they disagree with or are threatened by a teaching or commandment of a past prophet, they either dismiss the prophet altogether or selectively dismiss those teachings they find unsatisfactory.

I recall an account of a friend of mine who taught a Gospel Doctrine class decades ago in a small ward in the eastern United States (this occurred some time ago, and most of the ward members are no longer living). He frequently incorporated the teachings and prophecies of past Presidents of the Church into his lessons. The quotations dealt with subjects ranging from law and politics to science to various social issues. He told me that he was often challenged and sometimes outright mocked when he quoted past prophets because a few of the members of his class felt that relying on nineteenth-century Church leaders was outdated and naive. These members were prominent figures in the community—academics, politicians, bureaucrats, and business leaders who had become converted to the attitudes and wisdom of the world.

One member of the class even went so far as to declare, "Do you mean to tell us that you really believe every prophecy made by Church leaders will actually come to pass?" After my friend responded in the affirmative, the brother replied, "I am surprised that a man as educated as you would go that far!"

But despite this rather disturbing attitude, relying on the words of past prophets is not sentimental nonsense, nor naiveté, nor ignorance, nor foolishness. The words of past prophets stand firm and sound, independent of worldly scrutiny. And unless the living prophet amends them, they are just as authoritative as if the living prophet had spoken them today. As the Lord proclaimed, "For it shall come to pass, that which I spake by the mouths of my prophets shall be fulfilled" (D&C 42:39).

Our duty as Latter-day Saints is to decide whether we believe the Lord and have a testimony of His prophets. If we do, we must then choose to either benefit from following and sustaining those prophets or destroy ourselves through pride, rebellion, and disobedience. However, if we sustain our living prophet and those past prophets whose teachings still apply to us here and now, we can have assurance that we will enjoy safety, comfort, guidance, knowledge, and salvation.

Perhaps another reason some dismiss past prophets is responsibility. Because past teachings that are still in full force are binding on the Church, members are obligated to observe and obey them. However, they must first know and understand them. This requires purposeful study of the standard works, the writings and teachings of past Church presidents, and other readily available resources. For some, this demands much more study and personal initiative than what they are prepared to sacrifice.

Although studying the gospel involves effort, the benefits far outweigh the sacrifices. We can gain a greater knowledge of truth, which in turn gives us power in our lives to enjoy more of the Lord's blessings. Also, having access to greater truth and light dispels darkness and protects us more fully against the adversary and his attempts to deceive and destroy us.

In addition to the personal benefits, studying and following the teachings of past prophets is also required. We are under covenant as members of the Church to study, understand, and seek to live all the commandments. The Prophet Joseph Smith spent his ministry teaching this principle. He once stated, "It is impossible for a man to be saved in ignorance."[3] "A man is saved no faster than he gets knowledge. . . . Hence it needs revelation to assist us, and give us knowledge of the things of God."[4]

According to the Prophet, personal gospel knowledge is so essential because the "principle of knowledge is the principle of salvation. This principle can be comprehended by the faithful and diligent; and every one that does not obtain knowledge sufficient to be saved will be condemned."[5] He therefore admonished, "Wherefore, we again say, search the revelations of God; study the prophecies, and rejoice that God grants unto the world Seers and Prophets."[6]

The Savior commanded, "Search the prophets, for many there be that testify of these things" (3 Nephi 23:5).

The Prophet also stated that when "we take the sacred writings into our hands, and admit that they were given by direct inspiration for the good of man. We believe that God condescended to speak from the heavens and declare His will concerning the human family, to give them just and holy laws, to regulate their conduct, and guide them in a direct way, that in due time He might take them to Himself, and make them joint heirs with His Son."

However, the Prophet Joseph said that when we do admit that "the immediate will of heaven is contained in the Scriptures, are we not bound as rational creatures to live in accordance to all its precepts? Will the mere admission that this is the will of heaven ever benefit us if we do not comply with all its teachings? Do we not offer violence to the supreme intelligence of heaven, when we admit the truth of its teachings and do not obey them?"[7]

Even Nephi wrote about how indispensable gospel knowledge is when he penned, "I am left to mourn because of the unbelief, and the wickedness, and the ignorance, and the stiffneckedness of men; for they will not search knowledge, nor understand great knowledge, when it is given unto them in plainness, even as plain as word can be" (2 Nephi 32:7).

Each member of the Church must have a personal knowledge of gospel truths. And although it is not inappropriate to rely on others for some of our knowledge and learning, each member is an individual, an agent unto him or herself who cannot reach the celestial kingdom on "borrowed light." It was for this reason that the Prophet Joseph Smith commanded the Saints to "search the scriptures—search the revelations which we publish, and ask your Heavenly Father, in the name of His Son Jesus Christ, to manifest the truth unto you, and if you do it with an eye single to His glory, nothing doubting, He will answer you by the power of His Holy Spirit. You will then know for yourselves and not for another. You will not then be dependent on man for the knowledge of God; nor will there be any room for speculation. . . . Then again we say: Search the Scriptures, search the prophets and learn what portion of them belongs to you."[8]

The words of past prophets are extremely important. They are so important, in fact, that they remain binding on the Church. And unless the living prophet amends or repeals them, they are just as authoritative as if he had spoken them himself. Because of this, we as Latter-day Saints are obligated to know, believe, and sustain them.

Notes

1. Joseph Smith, *Teachings of the Prophet Joseph Smith,* sel. Joseph Fielding Smith

(Salt Lake City: Deseret Book, 1976), 22.

2. Joseph F. Smith, in Conference Reports of The Church of Jesus Christ of Latter-day Saints (Salt Lake City: The Church of Jesus Christ of Latter-day Saints, 1898 to present), October 1910, 4–5; emphasis added.
3. Smith, *Teachings,* 301.
4. Ibid., 217.
5. Ibid., 297.
6. Ibid., 12.
7. Ibid., 53–54.
8. Ibid., 11–12.

CHAPTER NINE

Benefits of Sustaining the Living Prophet

Because God loves each one of us, His work and glory is "to bring to pass the immortality and eternal life of man" (Moses 1:39). This is the reason He gives His children prophets: to bless them, guide them, and teach them the things they need to do to return to His presence and enjoy eternal life. Even when prophets deliver warnings or judgments against the wicked, they do so for the benefit and blessing of mankind. Elder Robert D. Hales stated, "There has always been a desperate need for the steady and reassuring voice of a living prophet of God: one who will speak the mind and will of God in showing the way to spiritual safety and personal peace and happiness."[1] As the Prophet Joseph Smith declared: "rejoice that God grants unto the world seers and prophets."[2]

President N. Eldon Tanner once stated, "In his infinite wisdom, and as part of the plan of life and salvation for his children, God has given us the blueprint to follow, the leadership to direct us and keep us on course, and the Church organization to help us lay the foundation and develop the skills, or make the preparation necessary, to lead us back to our eternal home. It is foolish to suppose that men can be left to their own devices and accomplish what God intended for them. That is just as unreasonable as it would be to leave a newborn babe on its own and expect it to learn to walk and talk and feed and clothe itself without assistance from those responsible for its care and training. A child so neglected and left alone would soon perish. So it is with us."[3]

The Blessings

Obedience and Sacrifice

Following and sustaining the living prophet does indeed entitle us to great blessings. First and foremost, it yields the blessings associated with obedience and sacrifice. If we hope to reap the blessings related to the living prophet, we must obey him. And obedience to God's representative is the only sure way to avoid the calamities reserved for the wicked and stiffnecked. The Prophet Joseph Smith taught that "on conditions of our obedience [God] has promised us great things."[4] This makes perfect sense since *all* blessings, rewards, benefits, and consequences result from adherence to a law. The Lord revealed, "There is a law, irrevocably decreed in heaven before the foundations of this world, upon which all blessings are predicated—And when we obtain any blessing from God, it is by obedience to that law upon which it is predicated" (D&C 130:20–21).

It follows then, that only by obeying the living prophet can we expect to enjoy the promised benefits. Further, we are blessed in direct proportion to the extent we obey. The greater our faith in and commitment to the prophet, the more the Lord blesses us. This is why King Benjamin taught that when you do what the Lord "hath commanded you . . . he doth immediately bless you" (Mosiah 2:24), because "the Lord in his great infinite goodness doth bless and prosper those who put their trust in him" (Helaman 12:1), which includes putting trust in His living prophet (D&C 1:38).

Associated with the law of obedience is the law of sacrifice. Anciently, this law involved animal sacrifice typifying the atonement of Christ. After Christ's resurrection and ascension to heaven, He required a different kind of sacrifice from His disciples: a broken heart and a contrite spirit. In other words, as Christ freely gave Himself for our salvation, He expects us to freely give ourselves to him—our will, our allegiance, our possessions, our lives. We must therefore sacrifice those opinions, preferences, and desires that conflict with His divine will, and in so doing, those that conflict with the living prophet as well. In essence, the Lord requires us to sacrifice our pride to sustain His representative, His mouthpiece.

The scriptures provide evidence of the blessings that accompany obedience and sacrifice to the living prophet. For example, after the children of Israel prayed for centuries for deliverance from bondage, the Lord sent them Moses—His living prophet—to free them from Egypt. Everyone who obeyed Moses by observing the Passover ordinances and placing lamb's blood on the lintels and posts of their doors was blessed immediately—not only by escaping the angel of death that night but also by gaining their freedom the next day. The Lord likewise blessed those who followed Enoch for obeying the living prophet of their day. Their obedience allowed them to overcome the tremendous wickedness of the world by living in a city that stood as one of the last safe havens on earth. Eventually, the Lord translated Enoch and his people because of their great faith and obedience.

In this dispensation, profound eternal blessings were bestowed on the Saints only as a result of their faith in, and obedience to, the living prophet. Building the Kirtland Temple, for example, required enormous faith and painful sacrifice. Many refused to heed the Prophet Joseph Smith when he commanded the Saints to build the temple as the Lord required. They didn't have sufficient faith to sustain the prophet when they realized what a burden constructing a temple would be. But those who trusted in the Prophet and committed themselves to the project enjoyed the blessings that followed.

The keys to seal families, gather Israel, lead the ten tribes from the North, and restore the gospel of Abraham were all given in the Kirtland Temple. The Savior appeared, as did an array of angels, prophets, and patriarchs from the other side of the veil. And both the temple and the surrounding community enjoyed an endowment that surpassed the day of Pentecost. A few years later, the Saints relied on the living prophet for their very survival. Had the Lord not given them a living prophet in Brigham Young (although he was not yet sustained president of the Church), no one would have benefited from the endowments given in the Nauvoo Temple, the organized exodus west, or the safety and prosperity of the Salt Lake Valley.

Our Sure Guide

Sustaining the prophet also provides a firm foundation upon which to build our lives and sure guidance with which to direct them. Few things, if any, in this life afford us real stability and lasting peace and happiness. Putting our complete trust in anything but God will eventually lead to disappointment and folly. "I will trust in [the Lord] forever," Nephi affirmed, "I will not put my trust in the arm of flesh; for I know that cursed is he that putteth his trust in the arm of flesh" (2 Nephi 4:34).

We must found our lives and the choices we make on truth—not the temporary or supposed truth the world offers, but eternal, unchanging truth that leads to safety. For "truth is knowledge of things as they are, and as they were, and as they are to come" (D&C 93:24). And since God is the only source of this truth, we must look to Him and to His living prophet for it, because "whatsoever is more or less than this is the spirit of that wicked one who was a liar from the beginning" (D&C 93:25).

In parable, Jesus discussed this firm foundation promised us through sustaining the prophet. He contrasted the wise and the foolish man—the first, who built his house upon the rock and the second, who built his on sand. When the storms of life (trials and adversities) began to blow, the house built on the rock "fell not" while the sandy foundation gave way and the foolish man's house collapsed. And to emphasize the point, Jesus added, "And great was the fall of it" (Matthew 7:24–27). Establishing one vital interpretation of this parable, the Prophet Joseph Smith taught that the rock to which Christ referred is revelation through a living prophet.[5]

A group of Westerners went on a hiking and climbing expedition into the Himalayan mountains. They hired an experienced Sherpa to take them through the dangerous and, to the group, unknown terrain. At first, the party followed their guide exactly, even going so far as to step exactly in his tracks. But soon, two of them decided they had learned enough from observation to take care of themselves. They walked just off to the side of the Sherpa's tracks because it gave them more room to maneuver. The guide tolerated this behavior for a time, but at a certain point in the hike he instructed the two men to fall back in line. After considerable objection, the renegades finally capitulated.

After a time, the Sherpa suddenly stopped. He gathered the party together, walked back from where they had just come, and tapped on the snow. To the party's shock, a large portion of the snow broke and fell hundreds of feet into the chasm below. The only part of the snow left was the narrow strip where the Sherpa had led the party. If the two renegades had continued to walk where they had been walking, they would have fallen through unstable ground and plummeted to their deaths.

This account is analogous to our following and sustaining the living prophet. Struggling with the Lord's oracle is as silly as arguing with the Sherpa. We are only wanderers on this earth, as unaccustomed to our heavenly or earthly environment as the party was in the Himalayas. The Sherpa not only knew his way through the mountains, but he also knew how to take others through safely. Likewise, the living prophet knows how to steer us clear of pitfalls, traps, and tragedies and how to lead us on the path of truth, life and salvation because the Lord has revealed it to him. From the Maker of the path, to the guide along the path, to us—the pathfinders—the Lord has prepared a sure and safe way for those who love Him and follow and sustain His guide, His living prophet.

Think of it—with all the inconsistencies, frailties, betrayal, lies, and turmoil in the world, we have at our disposal a direct channel to heaven upon which we can always rely for unwavering guidance and truth. The Lord Himself declared of His oracles, "The mouths of the prophets shall not fail" (D&C 58:8). However, we can only realize these blessings if we take advantage of them by listening, following, and sustaining the living prophet. The Lord promised that those who heed the words of the "holy prophets, who spake as they were inspired by the gift of the Holy Ghost, who truly testified of [Christ] in all things, should have eternal life" (D&C 20:26).

The Penalties

An effective way to understand the benefits of sustaining the prophet is to tackle the issue from the opposite point of view and consider the consequences of rejecting the living prophet. Although this topic may seem unpleasant and the discussion harsh, it nevertheless serves as a good reminder that no middle ground exists in the kingdom of God. In this case, we either sustain the living prophet and reap the benefits, or we reject him and face the consequences. Consider this idea as taught in the Doctrine and Covenants.

Curiously, the Lord introduces the Doctrine and Covenants to the world in a rather sober way. Instead of beginning by proclaiming the blessings available to mankind through the restored gospel in the latter days, He decries the wickedness of the world and warns of the destructions coming to the unrepentant. He proclaims that "they who will not hear the voice of the Lord, neither the voice of his servants, neither give heed to the words of the prophets and apostles, shall be cut off from among the people" of God (D&C 1:14).

Later, the Lord discussed Joseph Smith's place as the living prophet and admonished those "who receive the oracles of God" to "beware how they hold them lest they are accounted as a light thing, and are brought under condemnation thereby, and stumble and fall when the storms descend, and the winds blow, and the rains descend, and beat upon their house" (D&C 90:5). After detailing the horrific judgments reserved for the wicked in the last days, the Lord added, "There are none to deliver you; for ye obeyed not my voice when I called to you out of the heavens; ye believed not my servants, and when they were sent unto you ye received them not" (D&C 133:71).

Church history provides us with many accounts of the consequences of rejecting the living prophet. And these were applied both to individuals and to the Church as a whole. Mary Elizabeth Rollins Lightner, for example, recorded in her journal what the Prophet Joseph Smith prophesied concerning her and her family if they rejected him. She wrote that "with tears running down his cheeks he prophesied that if we left the Church we would have plenty of sorrow; that we would make property on the right and lose it on the left, we would have sickness on sickness, and lose our children; that I would have to work harder than I ever dreamed. . . . I thought these were very hard sayings . . . and I felt to doubt them. But the sequel proved them true. It all came to pass as he predicted."[6]

Another example of tragic consequences resulting from rejecting the living prophet is the Haun's Mill Massacre that occurred in Missouri in 1838. A mob ruthlessly attacked the Saints in this settlement and murdered several scores of its inhabitants. Although there was no excuse for this wicked and shameful act, the Prophet Joseph Smith had warned Brother Haun to move his people into the city for safety. When the counsel was refused, the Prophet had no choice but to allow them their agency. Sadly, rejecting the prophet's counsel resulted in needless tragedy.

In several instances, the general membership, collectively, were warned about the consequences of rejecting the living prophet. For example, speaking of the blessings promised to the Saints in relation to the Nauvoo Temple, the Lord warned: "If they will not hearken to my voice, nor unto the voice of these men whom I have appointed, they shall not be blest, because they pollute mine holy grounds and mine holy ordinances, and charters, and my holy words which I give unto them" (D&C 124:46).

This is one of the reasons sustaining the living prophet, the other General Authorities, and one's local leaders is an indispensable requirement for receiving a temple recommend. Warning us of the consequences of rejecting the Lord and His living prophet, the Prophet Joseph Smith declared:

> "O ye Twelve! And all Saints! Profit by this important Key—that in all your trials, troubles, temptations, afflictions, bonds, imprisonments and death, see to it, that you do not betray heaven; that you do not betray Jesus Christ; that you do not betray the brethren; that you do not betray the revelations of God . . . that ever was or ever will be given and revealed unto man in this world or that which is to come. In all your kicking and flounderings, see to it that you do not this thing, lest innocent blood be found upon your skirts, and you go down to hell."[7]

Further Revelation

I have often heard the sentiment expressed that the prophet and other General Authorities should teach the Church membership more truth and insight than what they have so far. Some want deeper doctrine, while others desire the Brethren to address pressing social problems or current political issues. While the living prophet may and has spoken about such things, and while past prophets have done so, it is true that we as a people do not generally receive much new doctrine or revelation from the General Authorities of the Church.

This of course begs the question, "Why not?" The answer is quite simple: we receive more revelation and instruction only when we are faithful to what has already been given. According to the Prophet Joseph Smith: "We cannot keep all the commandments without first knowing them, and we cannot expect to know all, or more than we now know unless we comply with or keep those we have already received."[8]

Mormon taught this principle in his account of the miraculous ministry of the Savior to the Nephites. He wrote:

> And now there cannot be written in this book even a hundredth part of the things which Jesus did truly teach unto the people;
>
> But behold the plates of Nephi do contain the more part of the things which he taught the people.
>
> And these things have I written, which are a lesser part of the things which he taught the people; and I have written them to the intent that they may be brought again unto this people, from the Gentiles, according to the words which Jesus hath spoken.

> And when they shall have received this, which is expedient that they should have first, to try their faith, and if it shall so be that they shall believe these things *then shall the greater things be made manifest unto them.*
>
> And if it so be that they will not believe these things, then shall the *greater things be withheld from them,* unto their condemnation (3 Nephi 26:6–10; emphasis added).

Mormon, who actually wrote to the Saints of this dispensation, taught several fundamental truths in this passage. First, the Lord gives knowledge to His people and tries their faith. Second, if they believe and are faithful, they will receive "greater things." Third, if they are not faithful to what was initially given, greater things are withheld. Fourth, they are under condemnation for treating lightly what was initially given.

Evidence of this pattern can be found in the Doctrine and Covenants, where the Lord commented on the condition of the Church. He declared to the Saints:

> And your minds in times past have been darkened because of unbelief, and because you have treated lightly the things you have received—which vanity and unbelief have brought the whole church under condemnation. And this condemnation resteth upon the children of Zion, even all. And they shall remain under this condemnation until they repent and remember the new covenant, even the Book of Mormon and the former commandments which I have given them, not only to say, but to do according to that which I have written—that they may bring forth fruit meet for their Father's kingdom; otherwise there remaineth a scourge and judgment to be poured out upon the children of Zion. (D&C 84:54–58)

Because the Lord felt the Saints had not lived up to former commandments and covenants, He was obliged to place them under condemnation until they remembered Him and their duties to Him more fully.

Speaking of why the Church does not receive more revelation from the Brethren than it does, Orson Pratt taught that it is "not because the Lord is not willing that his intelligent children should enjoy this greater amount of knowledge. . . . He is willing, on his part, that the people should become very intelligent in regard to everything, pertaining to their future welfare. He is willing that they should know more concerning himself, his attributes and their own, to learn concerning the glories of his kingdom and the mysteries thereof and everything that would be essential for their comfort and happiness in this world. This the Lord is willing to do. . . . But our present work is to comply with that which God has already given, and which he may hereafter give, through the living oracles that he has placed within our midst."[9]

It appears, then, that the key to receiving further instruction and revelation from the living prophet is clear. We must study what has already been given and do it. When we do, more will be given. When more is given, we need to listen and believe and be faithful to it. And when we do this, the Lord can more abundantly bless us temporally and spiritually and endow us with the sweet gifts that await us.

The Pitfall of Apostasy

What Is Apostasy?

Webster's Dictionary defines apostasy as "renunciation of a religious faith" or "abandonment of a previous loyalty." Although the Savior established His gospel in the New Testament, the world at large rejected His prophets and apostles and fell into the Apostasy, which lasted for 1700 years. This period officially ended when the Father and the Son appeared to Joseph Smith in the Sacred Grove in 1820. But while the Apostasy ended with the restoration of a living prophet to the earth, personal apostasy continues wherever anyone rejects the living prophet.

Discussing the principle of individual apostasy, the Prophet Joseph Smith taught, "I will give you one of the keys of the mysteries of the kingdom. It is an eternal principle, that has existed with God from all eternity: That man who rises up to condemn others, finding fault with the Church, saying that they are out of the way, while he himself is righteous, then know assuredly, that that man is in the high road to apostasy; and if he does not repent, will apostatize, as God lives."[10]

Of course, personal apostasy never starts with outward condemnation but, as with all behavior, thought and intent first. Several different internal reactions can lead to the outward expressions of apostasy. We can allow ourselves to become offended with a leader (justifiably or not), we can decide we know better than God's revealed word, or we can simply choose not to live the commandments. In short, apostasy begins whenever we set ourselves against the living prophet.

To further clarify the Prophet's definition of apostasy, the Church has characterized three distinct activities as apostate. The first is to "repeatedly act in clear, open, and deliberate public opposition to the Church or its leaders." The second is to "persist in teaching as Church doctrine information that is not Church doctrine after being corrected by bishops or higher authority." The third is to "continue to follow the teachings of apostate cults (such as those that advocate plural marriage) after being corrected by bishops or higher authority."[11] Let us discuss each of these in turn.

Acting in "clear, open, and deliberate public opposition to the Church or its leaders" qualifies a person as an apostate and can end in eventual excommunication (encouraging others to do this also qualifies as apostate activity). But publicly opposing Church leaders, especially the living prophet, like any harmful action, begins first with thought. Allowing these notions to stew gives them power and leads to a withdrawal of the Spirit, and in the absence of the Spirit we are left to our own imperfect reasoning and understanding. Such understanding, after harboring the belief that our leaders are wrong and we are right, will lead us to find fault with them at every turn. We will look for ways to justify our apostasy instead of ways to reverse our error, humble ourselves, sustain our leaders, and get the Spirit back into our lives. The terrible danger is that this cycle of apostasy feeds upon itself. I am reminded of a family who fell into this very trap. It started with the mother, who became annoyed when her son was required to wear a white shirt to pass the sacrament. Although at first she only expressed her disapproval at home, she began sharing her issue with ward members. She took exception, for example, with the fact that her husband—the recently released former bishop—never required the Aaronic priesthood youth to wear white shirts.

Soon she began finding fault with many of the bishop's decisions; she made sure to share her feelings with anyone who cared to listen. Eventually, her children publicly criticized the bishop, comparing him to their father and to the way things "used to be." Of course, they really had no basis to compare anything since they were only children, unaware of any supposed problem until their mother pulled them into her personal world of apostasy. The public criticism led to a conflict with the bishop and later the stake president, which prompted the father of this family to join the intrigue. Within a couple of years, the whole family had completely left the Church. Even when their friends and ward members attempted to love them and work with them, they vehemently refused contact with anyone or anything affiliated with their former membership. And though other issues may have contributed to their bitterness, the seeds of apostasy sprouted when the mother allowed herself to become offended over something as simple as wearing a white shirt.

But what if we truly feel a particular leader is wrong? The answer is, "It doesn't matter!" We can have more education, more experience in a particular calling, and be better liked by others—we can even claim to have received revelation that our leader is wrong. But the fact remains that we were not called to that position. The Lord honors His Church, His prophet, His priesthood, and all the callings that descend therefrom. As President Thomas S. Monson explained, "Whom the Lord calls, the Lord qualifies."[12] The Lord not only sustains those called to leadership positions in the kingdom, but He also recognizes and blesses those who sustain these leaders. Doing this brings us in harmony with the Lord and allows us access to the Holy Spirit. It opens a channel of living faith and power available only to those who faithfully uphold their leaders—regardless of personal feelings about their performance.

The second route to personal apostasy is to "persist in teaching as Church doctrine information that is not Church doctrine after being corrected by bishops or higher authority." I have a friend who learned this lesson the hard way. He joined the Church about the same time I did and quickly developed the same passion for doctrine and gospel knowledge. He became a great student of the scriptures and pored over the teachings of the Brethren.

After his mission, he was called to a teaching position in his home ward. He was an insightful and effective teacher, who always brought the Spirit to his class. On a particular occasion he was asked to meet with the bishop, who expressed concern about a couple of doctrines taught the previous Sunday. My friend explained the truth of the principles taught and even offered to reference them fully. His bishop had no interest in such an offer and expressed his discomfort with the inclusion of these doctrines in the class. Unfortunately, my friend was unsure about how to handle the situation. After all, he felt the doctrines were true, which entitled him to teach them. Eventually, after much consideration and introspection, he decided to respect his bishop's wishes.

This, of course, was the proper action to take. But it vexed my friend for some time. "Why shouldn't I be able to share these truths and insights?" he thought. Years later he discovered two profound answers to his question. The first was that if what he taught was not actually Church doctrine, the bishop, or any authority who presided over him, had the right to direct him to stop. The second was that even if the doctrine he taught was true, the bishop holds the keys to decide what will and will not take place in his ward. He has the right to set the bounds and limits because he has been placed in charge.

This is true whether the bishop is a great scriptorian or whether he knows little about the more advanced doctrines of the kingdom. And the same principle applies to other callings including stake, mission, and temple presidents. In order to serve the Lord and sustain the living prophet, our lives need to be in tune with the agenda of our leaders in areas where they have the right to preside. It doesn't matter, for example, that teaching a particular doctrine was acceptable to a previous leader; it only matters that it is acceptable to the current one. To stress again, doing this opens a channel of living faith and power available only to those who faithfully uphold their leaders.

The third way in which someone manifests personal apostasy is to "continue to follow the teachings of apostate cults after being corrected by bishops or higher authority." Everyone should understand that affiliating with a fanatical religious group is contrary to the gospel of Jesus Christ. But defining a cult only as a fringe religious organization is too narrow. Instead, one dictionary definition describes a cult merely as "a group or sect bound together by common beliefs." A more appropriate and inclusive standard to determine whether we are slipping into apostasy by affiliating with cults can be taken from the temple recommend interview. One of the questions asks if we affiliate with groups whose teachings are out of harmony with Church teachings. Therefore, anything—from a self-help guru, to a political organization, to a fan club—that encourages behavior or teaches principles out of harmony with the gospel and the living prophet, is considered by the Church to be apostate. And if we continue to affiliate with these we will find ourselves on the road to apostasy.

Opinion Is not Apostasy

Conflict with the living prophet and other priesthood leaders puts us out of favor with the Lord, but merely disagreeing with them may not necessarily rise to the level of apostasy. The Lord wants His people to be independent thinkers (of course, this liberty carries with it the responsibility of seeking the Spirit of revelation to ensure that our thinking conforms to the Lord's). Nevertheless, He places limits on acceptable individual expression. In 1869, President George Q. Cannon explained these limits, stating, "A friend . . . wished to know whether we . . . considered an honest difference of opinion between a member of the Church and the Authorities of the Church was apostasy. . . . We replied that we had not stated that an honest difference of opinion between a member of the church and the Authorities constituted apostasy for we could conceive of a man honestly differing in opinion from the Authorities of the Church and yet not be an apostate."

Qualifying this statement, President Cannon continued, "But we could not conceive of a man publishing these differences of opinion and seeking by arguments, sophistry and special pleading to enforce them upon the people to produce division and strife and to place the acts and counsels of the Authorities of the Church, if possible, in a wrong light, and not be an apostate, for such conduct was apostasy as we understood the term."[13]

Individuality and Sustaining the Living Prophet

Individuality Is Essential

Many people who find it difficult to follow the living prophet often feel that doing so means abandoning their individuality. They argue that those who sustain the prophet even at the expense of their own preferences and opinions become like mindless sheep who are asked to surrender their individuality and independence. But nothing could be further from the truth.

The beauty of our Heavenly Father's plan is that it relies on the principle of individuality. Speaking of the mysteries of eternity, the Lord revealed in one of the most profound sections of the Doctrine and Covenants: "All truth is independent in that sphere in which God has placed it, to act for itself, as all intelligence also; otherwise there is no existence" (D&C 93:30). Because independence, agency, and individuality are essential to all life and existence, the Lord always acts primarily with the individual in mind. In fact, the scriptures testify of this truth.

The Savior taught that even a sparrow cannot fall to the ground without Heavenly Father taking notice. He is, therefore, more mindful of each of His children, even so much that Jesus revealed, "The very hairs of your head are all numbered" (Matthew 10:29–31). One of the Master's great parables told of a shepherd who left his flock of ninety-nine sheep just to search for the lost one who had strayed from the fold. This parable, which speaks of those who have lost their way but are brought back to the gospel, pointedly describes the Lord's love of and concern for the individual. The account even reads that "he rejoiceth more of that sheep, than of the ninety and nine which went not astray" (Matthew 18:12–13).

Latter-day revelation confirms this focus on the individual. The Lord testified, "And how great is his [God's] joy in the soul that repenteth. . . . And if it so be that you should labor all your days in crying repentance unto this people, and bring, save it be one soul unto me, how great shall be your joy with him in the kingdom of my Father!" (D&C 18:13, 15).

The Prophet Joseph Smith declared: "Remember God sees the secret springs of human action, and knows the hearts of all living . . . God has respect to the feelings of His Saints . . ."[14] To clarify that salvation is ultimately an individual, personal matter, the Prophet also taught that "God judges men according to the use they make of the light which He gives them"[15] and does not simply lump them together as part of a church, a nation, a culture, or a family. President James E. Faust also spoke of the importance of individuality in the gospel of Jesus Christ. He taught, "All are equal before the Lord. Yet within our spiritual unity there is wide room for everyone's individuality and expression. In that setting, all are heirs to the kingdom of God."[16]

Individuality is so necessary to a personal relationship with God and salvation in His celestial kingdom that the Lord revealed He desires all persons to come to Him and know Him intimately—independent of any other earthly relationship. For He intends that "*every man* might speak in the name of God the Lord, even the Savior of the world" (D&C 1:20; emphasis added).

We never need fear that complete and absolute obedience and submission to the living prophet will rob us of our personality or individuality. On the contrary, sustaining the Lord's prophet gives us a depth and quality to our personality that we get no other way. And becoming one with the Lord allows us real independence from other forces and influences in the world that seek to destroy our distinctiveness and personal agency.

As we sustain the living prophet, even when it requires sacrifice, and avoid the pitfall of apostasy, we will enjoy the Lord's choice blessings. In the process, we will avoid the calamities the Lord reserves for the wicked and disobedient. We will have a ready guide, a firm foundation, and the peace of knowing we are led by a prophet of God.

Notes

1. Robert D. Hales, "Hear the Prophet's Voice and Obey," *Ensign,* May 1995, 15.
2. Joseph Smith, *Teachings of the Prophet Joseph Smith,* sel. Joseph Fielding Smith (Salt Lake City: Deseret Book), 1976, 12.
3. N. Eldon Tanner, "The Debate Is Over," *Ensign,* August 1979, 2.
4. Smith, *Teachings,* 19.
5. Ibid., 274.
6. Mary Elizabeth Rollins Lightner Smith, in Hyrum L. Andrus and Helen Mae Andrus, *They Knew the Prophet* (American Fork, Utah: Covenant Communications, 2004), 24.
7. Smith, *Teachings,* 156.
8. Ibid., 256.
9. Orson Pratt, in *Journal of Discourses,* 26 vols. (London: Latter-day Saints' Book Depot, 1854–86), 19: 9, 11.
10. Smith, *Teachings,* 156–57.
11. *General Handbook of Instructions* (Salt Lake City: The Church of Jesus Christ of Latter-day Saints, 1989), 10–3.
12. Thomas S. Monson, "You Make a Difference," *Ensign,* May 1988, 43.
13. George Q. Cannon, *Gospel Truth: Discourses and Writings of George Q. Cannon,* sel. Jerreld L. Newquist, 2 vols. (Salt Lake City: Deseret Book, 1974), 2:276–77.
14. Smith, *Teachings,* 19.
15. Ibid., 303.
16. James E. Faust, "Heirs to the Kingdom of God," *Ensign,* May 1995, 61.

CHAPTER TEN

How to Sustain the Living Prophet

I hope that the last chapter, "Benefits of Sustaining the Living Prophet," has proven informative, enlightening, and uplifting. But more important, it should motivate us all to commit more fully to sustain the living prophet. James tells us that "faith, if it hath not works, is dead" (James 2:17). In other words, knowledge without action is only potential. You may be excited about and dedicated to obeying and following the prophet, but you may be unsure about what to do next. This chapter will outline specific steps to help us fully sustain the Lord's living prophet and thereby reap benefits and blessings.

Seven Principles

First let us recap by outlining the seven principles essential to following the living prophet.

Principle 1—*Revelation and Commandments Are Given through the Living Prophet*

Prophets are an indispensable part of God's plan for directing His kingdom on earth and for blessing the lives of His children. Prophets are called to teach the people of the earth how to repent, come to Christ, and enter into the presence of God. As Amos taught, "Surely the Lord God will do nothing, but he revealeth his secret unto his servants the prophets" (Amos 3:7).

Principle 2—*The Living Prophet Is the Only Person Who Can Receive Revelation for the Church*

Although revelation is given to all who seek it with an honest heart, and there is no restriction on the amount of knowledge an individual may receive, the Lord speaks to His Church through His living prophet, and *only* through His living prophet. The prophet, therefore, has the authority to set the boundaries, limits, and parameters of all that is taught, said, and done in the Church. If a person acts or speaks beyond the bounds the living prophet has set, that person is out of harmony with the prophet and, therefore, out of harmony with the Lord.

Principle 3—*The Living Prophet Is Authorized to Give Revelation and Commandment on Any Subject*

Regardless of personal expertise or previous training, the living prophet is authorized to speak on any subject the Lord sees fit to have him speak on. Because the counsel or commandment comes originally from the Lord and not the prophet, we not only can have confidence in its value and truth, but we can also be assured that it is sound and sure.

Principle 4—*The Living Prophet Is Only a Prophet When He Speaks As a Prophet*

As a man, the living prophet possesses weaknesses and makes mistakes like any other mortal child of our Heavenly Father. Although we are not obligated to obey when he speaks as a man, he is a person of seasoned wisdom, intelligence, insight, honesty, integrity, and love. Even when he speaks as a man, his opinions are valuable and worthy of consideration. But when the living prophet speaks by the keys of his office and calling, his word is law to us because it is given as if the Lord Himself had spoken it.

Principle 5—*Other Church Leaders Are Authoritative Only When They Speak under the Direction of the Living Prophet*

The Twelve Apostles are prophets, seers, and revelators to the Church, but they are only authorized to act under the direction of the living prophet. Likewise, the other General Authorities and general presidencies speak authoritatively to the Church only under the same direction. Subsequently, all Church leaders—from stake presidents to Sunday School teachers—speak and act under the direction of, and through the keys of, the living prophet.

We are not under obligation to obey a commandment or believe a teaching of any Church leader if it is not sanctioned by or is out of harmony with the living prophet. However, the corollary is true: We are under covenant to obey and follow our Church leaders when they are in harmony with the living prophet and when their teachings and commandments are sanctioned by him.

Principle 6—*The Living Prophet's Words Are Preeminent over Past Prophets*

The teachings, actions, and commandments of past prophets are valuable, inherently true, and were given by revelation through priesthood keys, but they are secondary to what is or may be given by the living prophet. He is the person who has the right to set the bounds of what is taught and done—in the world and in the Church. Disregarding the living prophet to follow past prophets is to disregard them all. The living prophet is the Lord's one chosen representative on earth to whom we must look for life and salvation.

Principle 7—*If the Living Prophet Has Not Contradicted Past Teachings, They Are Still in Full Force*

The living prophet's words are preeminent over past prophets, but former commandments, doctrines, policies, and practices are still in full force if they have not been countermanded by the living prophet. Therefore, sustaining the living prophet means also sustaining past prophets and their teachings. We are not only under covenant to obey what has been given in the past, but we are also obligated to know what has been given in order to sustain it.

Following vs. Sustaining the Prophet

According to the dictionary, the word *sustain* means "to give support or relief to; to supply with sustenance; to allow or admit as valid; to confirm." Clearly then, *sustain* is an action word, not just an idea or philosophical concept. When we covenant to sustain the living prophet, we solemnly pledge to the Lord that we will do more than simply believe in the prophet's calling; we must do the things he asks of us.

Sustaining the prophet also means more than simply following him. To follow someone means to "come after," "be interested in," "observe or listen," or "go along with." We can follow the prophet and yet not truly sustain him. For example, we can comply with the commandments he gives but remain disgruntled about having to do so. We can acknowledge that the living prophet is the Lord's mouthpiece while consistently finding fault with him. Also, we can do the bare minimum of what is required of us but not do all we can to make the prophet's burdens lighter.

During the Nauvoo period, for example, the Prophet Joseph Smith was often unsure which of the Brethren he could trust. Although men like Sidney Rigdon, Frederick G. Williams, William Law, and others worked to carry out the Prophet's directives, they became troubled by a few doctrines and practices introduced by the Prophet. They continued to hold their offices and did not fully apostatize until later, but these leaders began to question and lose faith in the Prophet. They heeded him but only after struggling with him over issues they were uncomfortable with but that had already been settled by the Lord.

They taught the Saints to look to the Prophet Joseph Smith as the living prophet, yet many of their listeners could tell their hearts were not true to him. These leaders eventually refused to carry out some of his instructions and to teach doctrines he wanted taught. Thankfully, the Prophet could always rely on faithful men like Brigham Young, John Taylor, Heber C. Kimball, Wilford Woodruff, and others. But those who could not sustain the living prophet fully eventually found themselves in the midst of full apostasy, and many left the Church altogether.

Sustaining the prophet means more than just believing his words and obeying his counsel. It means fully supporting him in our hearts and through our words and deeds. The most outwardly apparent way we sustain the prophet is by raising our hands at conference as a sign of our sustaining vote. However, by doing so we acknowledge to the Lord—not just to the Brethren or to other Church members—that we will give our utmost to support, strengthen, encourage, uphold, confirm, and corroborate the living prophet.

The following are fundamental steps to take in order to sustain the prophet. There may be others, but these represent the essential ones needed to appropriately sustain the Lord's living oracle.

Obey the Prophet

The first, foremost, and most obvious way to sustain the living prophet is to obey him. President N. Eldon Tanner stated, "Wherever I go, my message to the people is: Follow the prophet."[1] Elder Robert D. Hales admonished, "Listen to a prophet's voice and obey. There is safety in following the living prophet."[2]

Nothing Is Trivial

A famous proverb states that a man never trips over a mountain but only on a stone. The meaning is quite clear: if ignored, the small, seemingly insignificant things in life will be our undoing, not usually the bigger, more obvious ones. This is profoundly true when we consider how crucial small and simple things are to making our way through this world. This especially applies in relation to living the gospel and sustaining the prophet.

Many people who refuse to fully sustain the prophet usually take issue with what they consider to be trivial things. They rationalize that because they are observing the big commandments, they are somehow justified in picking and choosing what they feel are the less-important things. However, every commandment is vital. As Jesus taught in the Sermon on the Mount: "Whosoever therefore shall break one of these least commandments, and shall teach men so, he shall be called the least in the kingdom of heaven: but whosoever shall do and teach them, the same shall be called great in the kingdom of heaven" (Matthew 5:19).

The scriptures offer many examples of how individuals rose or fell because of small, seemingly insignificant things. The book of 2 Kings 5 records the account of Naaman, a Syrian of some prominence who sought out the prophet Elisha to cure his leprosy. Instead of relying on a stunning overture of miraculous power, Elisha took a more subtle approach. He commanded Naaman to wash seven times in the Jordan River to be cured. Sadly for Naaman, his pride prevented him from following Elisha's direction because of its simplicity. When he was finally convinced to heed the prophet, the apparently trivial act instantly healed him of an otherwise incurable disease.

Sampson illustrated the opposite end of the spectrum. His Nazarite covenant restricted him from cutting his hair. In return, the Lord maintained Sampson's great strength and blessed him with victory over his enemies. As simple a thing as this was, it appeared to be the linchpin that held Sampson together and by which he met his downfall.

The Book of Mormon records the problem the Israelites had with seemingly insignificant things after they left Egypt. During their journey through the wilderness, the Lord punished their wickedness by afflicting them with poisonous serpents. However, He also prepared a way for them to escape their punishment. They just needed to look upon a brazen serpent held up by Moses and be healed. But Nephi explained that many of them perished "because of the simpleness of the way" the Lord chose to heal them (1 Nephi 17:41).

Obviously, the smallest of commandments are important and must be observed. Perhaps it seems that some of the prophet's words or directions are trivial and have little to do with eternal salvation. However, the commandment itself is often less important than the test of obedience to that commandment that can make or break us. As the Lord stated: "Wherefore, be not weary in well-doing, for ye are laying the foundation of a great work. And out of *small things* proceedeth that which is great. Behold, the Lord requireth the heart and a willing mind; and the willing and obedient shall eat the good of the land of Zion in these last days" (D&C 64:33–34; emphasis added).

In this way especially, little things are so crucial. Pride and unwillingness to obey are the only real trivial things in our lives. In the final analysis, refusing to heed the living prophet, especially in so-called trivial matters, yields no real benefit; no one ever really gains anything of value. And compared to the loss of blessings and the loss of the Spirit that accompany opposition to the Lord's anointed, it seems foolish not to take advantage of the opportunity of doing so very little and gaining so very much.

Addressing the Saints at the conclusion of general conference, President David O. McKay explained that there is "no one great thing that we can do to obtain eternal life, and it seems to me that the great lesson to be learned in the world today is to apply in the little acts and duties of life the glorious principles of the gospel. Let us not think that because some of the things named this afternoon may seem small and trivial, that they are unimportant. Life, after all, is made up of little things. Our life, our being, physically, is made up here of little heart beats. Let that little heart stop beating, and life in this world ceases."[3] As one notable leader aptly stated, "Big problems grow out of thinking that little things don't matter."[4]

Follow, But Not Blindly

Believing and sustaining the prophet even if we do not always understand why at first does not mean we are weak-willed or that we have abandoned a personal testimony of the truth. We are not only permitted to receive a personal witness but are also required to do so. Teaching this principle to the Saints, President Brigham Young testified:

> I am more afraid that this people have so much confidence in their leaders that they will not inquire for themselves of God whether they are led by him. I am fearful they settle down in a state of blind self-security, trusting their eternal destiny in the hands of their leaders with a reckless confidence that in itself would thwart the purposes of God in their salvation, and weaken that influence they could give to their leaders, did they know for themselves, by the revelations of Jesus, that they are led in the right way. Let every man and woman know, by the whispering of the Spirit of God to themselves, whether their leaders are walking in the path the Lord dictates, or not.[5]

At first reading, this quotation may seem to encourage disagreeing with the living prophet. Some might even argue that we have a duty to criticize our priesthood leaders and encourage them to change to conform with our opinions and desires. However, this is not what President Young suggested. A closer reading of this passage reveals that the proper course of action instead is to automatically trust and sustain the living prophet (and therefore our other priesthood leaders as well) and then pray for a personal witness of the truth in our own hearts by the Holy Ghost. If we feel that our opinions or preferences are not in harmony with what has been given, we have an even greater responsibility to seek the Lord for a personal witness and understanding of the issue. In this way we retain our individuality while reaping the blessings of unity with the Lord and His living prophet.

Surrendering Our Will

The gospel plan relies on individuality and requires us not to follow our leaders blindly. The Lord desires His children to think and act for themselves and not simply respond to programming like robots. However, this does not mean we should think, believe, or act in any manner we wish. And although the Lord will never violate agency by compelling a person to obey Him, the only real way to achieve salvation is to put His will first in all things and to bend our will to conform to His.

As Jacob admonished, "Wherefore, my beloved brethren, reconcile yourselves to the will of God, and not to the will of the devil and the flesh" (2 Nephi 10:24). The Prophet Joseph Smith likewise taught, "As a Church and a people, it behooves us to be wise, and to seek to know the will of God, and then be willing to do it."[6]

As a sinless being, Christ set the perfect example for surrendering personal will to the Father's will. For example, He encapsulated the very essence of His gospel in the phrase, "I came into the world to do the will of my Father, because my Father sent me" (3 Nephi 27:13). Abinadi taught that although Christ was the Creator and Lord of heaven and earth, He "suffere[d] himself to be mocked, and scourged, and cast out, and disowned by his people" and "crucified, and slain, the flesh becoming subject even unto death, the will of the Son being swallowed up in the will of the Father" (Mosiah 15:5, 7). Thus, Christ could say to the Nephites when He appeared to them, "I have drunk out of that bitter cup which the Father hath given me, and have glorified the Father in taking upon me the sins of the world, in the which I have suffered the will of the Father in all things from the beginning" (3 Nephi 11:11).

Think of it: the Firstborn and Only Begotten of the Father, who never committed sin and who had all power in heaven and on earth at His disposal, loved and trusted His Heavenly Father so perfectly that He surrendered His will to the will of the Father in all things—and at all costs. The submission of personal will to perform the Atonement was so intense, in fact, that the Savior spoke of it in these words:

> For behold, I God, have suffered these things for all, that they might not suffer if they would repent; but if they would not repent they must suffer even as I; Which suffering caused myself, even God, the greatest of all, to tremble because of pain, and to bleed at every pore, and to suffer both body and spirit—and would that I might not drink the bitter cup, and shrink—Nevertheless, glory be to the Father, and I partook and finished my preparations unto the children of men. . . . I am Jesus Christ; I came by the *will of the Father,* and *I do his will.* (D&C 19:16–19, 24; emphasis added)

Clearly, Christ personally preferred to avoid suffering the pains of the Atonement. Nevertheless, He set the standard of obedience, love, and submission of ego for all to follow.

We also have examples of prophets who learned to surrender their wills and personal desires to the Lord. In opposition to what appeared to be common sense and moral, Abraham willingly reconciled himself to sacrifice his son, Isaac, in obedience to God's command. Although this was only a test, Abraham learned how to consecrate all things to the Lord if required.

President Heber C. Kimball faced his own Abrahamic test in this dispensation. In addition to accepting the covenant of plural marriage that contradicted every personal instinct he had, Heber was tested even further. The Prophet Joseph Smith told Heber that the Lord required him to give up his sweetheart, Vilate, to be sealed to the Prophet instead. With commitment to Christ and faith in His living prophet, Heber surrendered his will to the will of the Lord. Like Abraham, Heber was relieved when he discovered that his ordeal was only a test, but he was also overjoyed knowing that he had the integrity to remain faithful to the Lord's living prophet.

The need to sacrifice all things and completely submit one's will to the Lord's is not required of prophets only. The Prophet Joseph Smith (who had his own share of Abrahamic tests) taught, "The sacrifice required of Abraham in the offering up of Isaac, shows that if a man [or woman] would attain to the keys of the kingdom of an endless life; he must sacrifice *all things*."[7] The Lord made it clear that all the Saints "must needs be chastened and tried, even as Abraham, who was commanded to offer up his only son" (D&C 101:4).

To those who do not understand the nature of man's relationship to God, the idea of surrendering one's will to another person—especially the way Abraham or Heber C. Kimball did—is appalling. And agreeably, doing such a thing is morally reprehensible and destroys individuality—*if* a person were surrendering his will to anyone other than a perfect, omnipotent, omniscient, all-loving God who acts only in the best interest of His children.

But rather than being an act of perversion and degradation, sacrificing our will to do the will of our Father in Heaven is a life-affirming, ennobling, and purifying experience that brings us closer to Him and enables us to become like Him. Instead of losing everything we have and are, surrendering our will allows us to become who we truly want to be.

Teaching this principle, Elder Neal A. Maxwell stated, "But is being consecrated and 'swallowed up' a threat to our individuality? No! Heavenly Father is only asking us to lose the old self in order to find the new and the real self. It is not a question of losing our identity but of finding our true identity!"[8] President Joseph F. Smith argued that consecrating our will to God, rather than being a sign of weakness and lack of individuality, shows a "stronger characteristic of individuality for men and women to bring themselves into harmony and union with the purposes of the Almighty than to be divided against them or separate from them."[9]

Perhaps our unwillingness to surrender our will has less to do with individuality and more to do with something else. Elder Maxwell explained, "So many of us are kept from eventual consecration because we mistakenly think that, somehow, by letting our will be swallowed up in the will of God, we lose our individuality. What we are really worried about, of course, is not giving up self, but selfish things—like our roles, our time, our preeminence, and our possessions. No wonder we are instructed by the Savior to lose ourselves. . . . Ironically, so many people already lose themselves anyway in their consuming hobbies and preoccupations but with far, far lesser things."[10]

Following the Lord and receiving His blessings requires surrendering our will to Him. And a great part of that process involves surrendering our will to the counsel and commandments of His living prophet. Don't worry if your opinions or preferences conflict with the living prophet—just let go and have faith that the Lord knows what He is doing and is mindful of you and all His children.

Don't fret if the popular attitude of the day or your education, family, cultural background, and traditions conflict with what the living prophet teaches or admonishes; just surrender your will and stop struggling. The Lord tests us to prove whether we will follow Him in all things—including sustaining His prophet. And when we demonstrate that we will, we grow spiritually, and He immediately blesses us according to our faith and obedience.

An Explanation Is Not Necessary

Sometimes it is difficult to sustain the prophet and obey the commandments he gives. Rather than getting discouraged, we need to take comfort in the fact that such challenges are part of the plan. As earthly children of our Heavenly Father, we have been voluntarily placed in a mortal probation (what the scriptures call the "second estate") and have had a veil placed over our minds so we forget all that we knew and were in the pre-earth life.

This requires us to walk by faith through this probationary state. This is the only way we can truly grow and develop spiritually, and it is the only way we can properly be proved. Obstacles all around us pose threats to our progression and salvation, but we have been given the capacity to overcome them through faith, hard work, and agency. Whether we were born in the covenant or have found the gospel later in life, we all have similar tests and trials, including obedience to the commandments and to the Lord's living prophet.

Perhaps the most difficult aspect of sustaining the prophet is believing and obeying his words when we do not understand them or why they are given. This is most definitely a test of our faith. Of course, the purpose of mortal probation is to be tested to see if we will be obedient in all things in order to develop our faith (Abraham 3:25). We must, therefore, learn to always sustain the prophet, even without necessarily knowing the reason or the outcome.

This is a much more daunting task if we are not fully converted to the fact that direction and commandment do not ultimately come from the prophet but rather from the Lord. Because of the Lord's infinite knowledge and wisdom, and because He requires of us only things that will result in our benefit and happiness, we can have confidence obeying Him and His living prophet.

However, this requires two things of us—trust and love. We need to trust that the Lord knows what He is doing, trust that the prophet is truly speaking for the Lord, and trust ourselves that we are secure enough to obey without always having to understand every reason for obeying. And in order to completely trust anyone, we must love that person and know that he loves us and has nothing but our best interest at heart.

The scriptures provide glowing examples of this kind of trust and love. Adam and Eve did not reject the Lord after He exiled them to the lone and dreary world. Instead, our first parents humbly obeyed the commandment to offer sacrifices without understanding the purpose. Abraham consecrated all he had to the Lord, even when that required taking the life of his son Isaac—the miracle child through whom Abraham's covenant was to be perpetuated. To the average person this would seem not only questionable but also insane. It seems to fly in the face of all common sense and reason. Yet Abraham loved and trusted God and knew that His motives were pure. He willingly obeyed and was blessed beyond mortal comprehension for passing the test of his faith.

No matter how much Job suffered, he never forsook the Lord, and he acknowledged a higher purpose in his afflictions, proclaiming that God "knoweth the way that I take: when he hath tried me, I shall come forth as gold" (Job 23:10). Paul had his own share of suffering in the service of the Lord. But after submitting to beatings, shipwrecks, and imprisonment, he testified that "in all these things we are more than conquerors through him that loved us. For I am persuaded, that neither death, nor life, nor angels, nor principalities, nor powers, nor things present, nor things to come, nor height, nor depth, nor any other creature, shall be able to separate us from the love of God, which is in Christ Jesus our Lord" (Romans 8:37–39).

Some might argue that the experience of Paul or Job or Abraham differs from anything we might expect to experience because God, and not another mortal person, commanded them. However, consider the experience of Nephi. He had just fled Jerusalem because wicked men sought his father's life. While in the wilderness, his family took every step necessary to avoid being discovered by anyone. Just as Nephi expected to travel farther away from his home, Lehi informed him that the Lord had commanded him and his brothers to return to Jerusalem—into the very heart of danger!

If this were not bad enough, Nephi was also told to obtain the valuable and highly coveted brass plates from a wicked man who had the political and military power to destroy his entire family at the snap of a finger. With a fairly comprehensive knowledge of the gravity of the situation, Nephi still had the faith and integrity to utter these sublime words: "I will go and do the things which the Lord hath commanded, for I know that the Lord giveth no commandments unto the children of men, save he shall prepare a way for them that they may accomplish the thing which he commandeth them" (1 Nephi 3:7).

What a remarkable response to the command of the Lord's prophet. Nephi did not receive the call to go to Jerusalem directly from the Lord but instead was informed through a mortal, imperfect representative. More to the point, the representative was his own father—the one person children are often most inclined to ignore. But because of the sacrifices he had made in his life up to that point, Nephi had developed the faith sufficient to know several important things. He knew that the Lord loved him and would never do anything that was not in his best interest, he knew that his father loved him and acted with similar regard, he knew that his father was indeed a prophet of God, and he knew that the Lord would never give a commandment without providing a way to fulfill it.

Perhaps some would still argue that applying this situation to the average Latter-day Saint is unfair because Nephi was an extraordinary person who had a prophet for a father and was being prepared to become a prophet himself. Let us turn then to yet another account from the scriptures. Because of Israel's continual wickedness after the death of King Solomon, the Prophet Elijah cursed the land with a drought, resulting in a dreadful famine throughout the land.

During this time of scarcity and suffering, the Lord commanded Elijah to go to a widow and ask to be fed. The widow, who was just preparing to use up the last of her food when Elijah arrived, welcomed the prophet into her home. Elijah declared to the destitute woman, "Fear not; go and do as thou hast said: but make me thereof a little cake first, and bring it unto me, and after make for thee and for thy son. For thus saith the Lord God of Israel, the barrel of meal shall not waste, neither shall the cruse of oil fail, until the day that the Lord sendeth rain upon the earth" (1 Kings 17:13–14).

With faith in the Lord and faith in His living prophet, the widow obeyed in the face of contrary human wisdom and gave the last of her food to Elijah. And although Elijah's words were all fulfilled and the woman and her house "did eat many days" (1 Kings 17:15), it took enormous faith to obey at all costs without knowing absolutely the purpose behind her sacrifice or how things would turn out.

The Prophet Joseph Smith often tested the faith of the Saints by asking them to do things that at times seemed outrageous or ridiculous. He did so, of course, because he loved them and desired to stretch their faith and obedience to him as the living prophet. One such instance occurred in Nauvoo. The Prophet walked into Edwin Woolley's store and commanded him to box up all his goods, explaining that they were needed by the Church. The Prophet gave no justification. Committed to the Lord and His living prophet, Edwin did as Joseph commanded. When the Prophet saw that Brother Woolley had passed the test, he instructed him to put his goods back on the shelves.[11] And though many Saints were not as true to the Prophet, many were and proved their trustworthiness and obedience time and again without needing to immediately know the reasons.

We may experience situations when we are asked or commanded by the living prophet to do things without understanding why or what the consequences may be, but we need to be prepared to sacrifice our selfishness, our pride, and our limited reason and logic and trust that the Lord and His prophet will never ask us to do anything that is not in our ultimate best interest. And though we may decide that a particular thing is not best for us, the Lord's wisdom far exceeds our own, as does His infinite love, mercy, and blessings. As the Prophet Joseph Smith taught, "Whatever God requires is right, no matter what it is, although we may not see the reason thereof until long after the events transpire."[12]

Keep the Commandments

The standard works, the teachings of past prophets, the teachings of the living prophet, and revelation from the Holy Ghost all testify that the simplest way to sustain the prophet is also the best way to follow the Lord: keep the commandments! In the most plain and sublime terms, Jesus taught, "If ye love me, keep my commandments" (John 14:15). In this dispensation, He taught, "Blessed is he that keepeth my commandments, whether in life or in death; and he that is faithful in tribulation, the reward of the same is greater in the kingdom of heaven" (D&C 58:2). However, the Lord reiterated this idea in sharper terms, testifying, "Not every one that saith unto me, Lord, Lord, shall enter into the kingdom of heaven; but he that doeth the will of my Father which is in heaven" (Matthew 7:21).

In his famous discourse, King Benjamin taught the simple and singular importance of obeying the commandments. He proclaimed, "All that he [the Lord] requires of you is to keep his commandments; and he has promised you that if ye would keep his commandments ye should prosper" (Mosiah 2:22). The Prophet Joseph Smith commanded the Saints to "live in strict obedience to the commandments of God, and walk humbly before Him."[13] He further stated, "I spoke to the people, showing them that to get salvation we must not only do some things, but *everything* which God has commanded. Men may preach and practice everything except those things which God commands us to do, and will be damned at last. . . . The object . . . is to obey and teach others to obey God in what He tells us to do."[14]

It may be disheartening to hear that each of us must live all of the commandments, but it should be relieving to know that we are not required to live them perfectly all at once here on this earth. We simply need to do all we can with what we have been given. We need to be willing to obey perfectly if we could do so, all the while working to overcome those weaknesses that keep us from perfection.

Even though this might seem to some like an excuse to sin, it is not. Nor is it a way to rationalize away living the commandments. The Lord can bless the weak, imperfect, and sinful as well as those who are completely righteous. Section 46 of the Doctrine and Covenants expresses this sentiment beautifully. First the Lord discusses the gifts of the Spirit—the manifestations of which are a true indication of a person's purity and faith. The Master states that these gifts "are given for the benefit of those who love me and keep *all my commandments,*" but then he adds the relieving addendum, "*And him that seeketh so to do;* that *all* may be benefited that seek or that ask of me" (D&C 46:9; emphasis added).

The Prophet Joseph Smith explained that no one was "ever perfect but Jesus: And why was He perfect? Because He was the Son of God, and had the fullness of the Spirit and greater power than any man. But notwithstanding their vanity, men look forward with hope . . . to the time of their deliverance."[15]

With this in mind, then, let us sustain the prophet by keeping the commandments as perfectly as we are able, with a desire in our hearts to keep them all. And let us commit to obey whatever has come from the mouth of our prophets as well as whatever may come in the future.

Sustain All Other Leaders

Keys and Stewardship

While I was teaching a Gospel Principles class, an investigator asked me to explain the prophet's role and responsibilities. As I set about answering the woman's question, I included the fact that the prophet is the president of the Church and, as such, holds the keys to preside over the entire Church. He is also the Lord's mouthpiece and living revelator to the Saints and to the world. This is a worthy description of the prophet's role, power, and duties, but I did not realize until years later that my description was incomplete and the office of the living prophet involved fundamentally more than I ever thought at that time.

The living prophet is indeed the president of the Church. He is the only person on earth at a given time who holds all the keys of the kingdom. The prophet does more than just preside over the Church as a whole; the keys he holds empower him to preside over every calling in the Church. It is appropriate to say, then, that in the ultimate sense, the president of the Church is the president of every stake, the bishop of every ward, the president of every Relief Society, the president of every Primary and Young Men/Young Women organization, and the head of every seminary and institute program, and so on.

However, the prophet is just one man; he could not possibly fulfill all the callings for which he holds keys. Because of this, the Lord has instituted a stewardship program to assist the prophet and help the Church run efficiently. Other Church members are called to preside over various positions under the direction and authority of the president of the Church. When they are set apart for this, the keys pertaining to their particular calling are temporarily lent out to them by the living prophet, just as his keys are lent to him by the Lord, to whom they rightly belong. However, the ultimate earthly responsibility and authority for them always remains with the president of the Church.

Because of this stewardship arrangement, those who hold callings in the Church not only have the right to preside in positions of authority, but they also represent the living prophet and stand vicariously in his place when exercising the keys of their callings. And because they represent the living prophet, they ultimately represent the Lord. This is an awesome and sacred responsibility—one that we need to understand and cherish. It needs to be understood and cherished by those holding callings in the Church, as well as by those who are presided over by those callings. For example, a bishop must fulfill his calling with humility, love, integrity, and concern for the welfare of his ward members because he operates under the direction of the Lord Jesus Christ and the living prophet. In a very real sense, he stands as their direct representative to his ward. The keys he holds belong to them and must never be used in anger or arrogance, or to satisfy his pride and ambition.

By this same token, however, this bishop's ward members must realize that because his keys come from the Lord Jesus Christ through the living prophet, he is empowered to act and to speak on their behalf. This means that his ward members need to treat his calling with the same respect they would if the prophet himself were sitting every Sunday on the stand.

And this same attitude applies to any position of authority or leadership in the Church. Each leader operates under the direction of the Lord and His living prophet, temporarily borrowing keys to officiate in a particular calling. Therefore, each leader literally stands in place of the Lord and the prophet to those over whom they have stewardship. Because of this relationship, we all must treat our leaders with respect. When they ask us to do something (so long as it pertains to their particular stewardship), we are as obligated to heed them as if the living prophet had given the direction.

Although not every leader in the Church measures up to the quality of character and ability of the living prophet, we are still obligated to obey our leaders notwithstanding their imperfections and weaknesses. Even if we do not care for the person, we need to respect the calling because the Lord himself does; and each calling is only an extension of the office of the living prophet. Another important thing to keep in mind is that with authority comes responsibility and accountability. All leaders in the Church will one day give an accounting of how they fulfilled their stewardships. If a person fails to fulfill a calling, the Lord will deal with that person in His own way and in His own time. He merely asks us to sustain the office (in righteousness) regardless of our feelings about the person.

Priesthood Authority and Abuse of Power

Because the power, authority, and keys of the living prophet are so comprehensive, some may feel uneasy about the potential for being taken advantage of, manipulated, or abusively controlled. Although this is a concern many have felt before, we must ask ourselves three questions: (1) Is this the Lord's Church? (2) Would He ever let it be led astray? (3) Do I have a personal testimony that the living prophet is called of God? If we have the faith, to whatever degree we are able, to answer affirmatively to these questions, we can feel secure in the doctrine that the living prophet presides over every calling and over every member and that we must all sustain him no matter what he requires.

President Brigham Young taught, "The Lord Almighty leads this Church, and he will never suffer you to be led astray if you are found doing your duty. You may go home and sleep as sweetly as a babe in its mother's arms, as to any danger of your leaders leading you astray, for if they should try to do so the Lord would quickly sweep them from the earth. Your leaders are trying to live their religion as far as [they are] capable of doing so."[16]

President Wilford Woodruff likewise declared, "I say unto Israel, the Lord will never permit me or any other man who stands as President of the Church to lead you astray. . . . It is not the program. It is not the mind of God."[17]

Indeed, the Lord will never allow the living prophet to lead the Church astray. However, just because the prophet presides over every calling does not mean that every person holding a calling is as spiritually sound as the president of the Church. And although this Church is filled with wonderful, faithful, sincere, hardworking Saints who strive to do the Lord's will and fulfill their callings, sadly, a few members from time to time abuse their authority.

Nevertheless, this is in no way a problem running rampant in the Church today. Instead, such situations occur in rare cases when compared to the large membership of the Church and the hundreds of thousands of callings held by its members. Further, we must not erroneously link individual mistakes and abuses to the living prophet or the priesthood in general. The priesthood and all callings, keys, powers, and authority center on Jesus Christ and are given to men by Him. To disparage the priesthood is to disparage Christ Himself.

But because agency is also a gift of God, He sometimes allows men to work out their own salvation or damnation by tolerating their unrighteous use of His authority until they either repent or He removes them. The Old Testament provides a good example of this. Although Saul was a righteous man when Samuel anointed him king of Israel, he allowed himself to succumb to wickedness. Nevertheless, the Lord, according to His own design, suffered Saul to remain king. Even when he sought David's life because of jealousy, Saul remained in power, and David refused to raise "his hand against the Lord's anointed" (1 Samuel 26:9). When the Lord had fulfilled His purposes, He took Saul and replaced him with David.

Other instances of the Lord tolerating unrighteousness in His priesthood holders come from the Book of Mormon. For example, when Lehi's family experienced hardship in the wilderness after Nephi broke his bow, even Lehi, a prophet of God, lost faith and joined his wicked sons in their murmuring. Instead of assuming leadership of the clan, Nephi humbly approached his father for a solution to the family's predicament, deferring to his authority and reminding him of his obligation before the Lord.

Because the Lord sometimes tolerates abuse of His priesthood does not mean such abuse should always be tolerated. The Lord most often works through others to accomplish His purposes, and He expects us as members of the Church and watchmen in Israel to "see that there is no iniquity in the church" (D&C 20:54). Remember, President Young promised that the Lord "will never suffer you to be led astray if you are found doing your duty."[18] And our duty as members is to watch over the Church and each other. Therefore, if a serious abuse occurs, it should always be reported to proper priesthood leaders.

This is one of the reasons a hierarchy of priesthood offices exists. If something is awry with a leader in relation to his stewardship, he is accountable to the next leader up the chain. That leader likewise answers to the steward who presides over him, and so forth all the way to the president of the Church. But priesthood leaders most often do not know about abuses and therefore can do nothing about them if they are kept secret.

Church members should not make a mad dash for their bishop or stake president's offices to report an alleged abuse. Wisdom and discretion must prevail when deciding to report an abuse of priesthood authority. For instance, a conflict of personality is not an abuse of power. Although our goal is to be "of one heart and one mind" (Moses 7:18), each of us is imperfect and prone to discord based on nothing but differing preferences, opinions, and dispositions. Even if a priesthood leader's behavior could be characterized as miserable, cranky, or rude, it probably does not rise to the level of abuse.

The key to determining whether a leader is abusing his authority can be discovered in one question: "Is this leader acting within the scope of his calling?" If the answer is yes, then no abuse exists. If the answer remains unclear, seek the Spirit to determine whether to report an abuse. But even if you dislike the way the leaders fulfill their callings, the discretion is theirs as long as they do not overstep their bounds.

Holding the priesthood, or any calling of authority or leadership in the Church, is a difficult thing. Callings demand love, discipline, patience, revelation, integrity, faith, and many other Christlike attributes. No one is perfect—from the prophet, to the least member of the kingdom. We ought to be as humble, helpful, patient, and forgiving as possible (without allowing abuses to occur) where our leaders are concerned.

Again, do not go running to priesthood leaders every time your feelings get hurt about how you were treated. And in those instances when rare abuses have gone unchecked or overlooked, we can find solace in the truth that the Church is overflowing with good and faithful leaders, the Lord will never allow the living prophet to lead us astray, and God "will mete out a just recompense of reward upon the heads of all [your] oppressors" (D&C 127:3).

Shoulder to the Wheel

As we follow and sustain our Church leaders, who work on behalf of the living prophet, we need to roll up our proverbial sleeves and go to work in the kingdom. The Lord declared, "I give unto you a commandment, that every man, both elder, priest, teacher, and also member, go to with his might, with the labor of his hands, to prepare and accomplish the things which I have commanded" (D&C 38:40). If we are asked to fulfill a calling, to do a job, or even informally lend a hand from time to time, we need to have a willing heart and do what we are asked. When we hesitate to take a calling or fulfill an assignment because we cannot be bothered, it is as if we were looking straight into the prophet's face and telling him no.

I was privileged to spend a summer in what I consider to be one of the most paradisiacal places on earth. During that summer, I attended a small branch of the Church and met some wonderful, faithful Saints. Because it was such a small branch, everyone had to pitch in for things to run smoothly. In fact, some members had three or four callings.

I remember being impressed with a brother I met that summer. He was a kind and down-to-earth person who was extremely friendly and charismatic. He spoke intelligently and with conviction about the gospel. I was especially impressed with the magnificent family he and his wife were raising. When I asked a friend in the branch what calling this brother held, I was surprised to learn that he held none. Not wanting to gossip but curious why he had no calling, I inquired of my friend further.

I was told that no gossip was necessary; the man made no secret of the fact that he refused to accept any callings in the Church because he felt that his family came first and that attending to a calling would take too much time away from family (how is that for rationale!). Even when several branch presidents over the years had explained that callings are a natural part of Church membership and that he was called though priesthood channels, he still refused.

This is a shining example of not sustaining the prophet by refusing to follow priesthood leaders and refusing to dig in and build the kingdom. Perhaps if this brother had really been converted to sustaining the living prophet and understood all that it involved, he might have chosen differently. It is almost certain, however, that if the prophet stood toe-to-toe with this brother and extended a calling personally, he would not have been quite so bold about refusing to serve.

Avoid Worldly Pitfalls

Zion vs. Babylon

During this earth's six thousand years of temporal existence, the Lord has always attempted to gather His people Israel out of the wickedness of the world to teach them "of his ways" and to "walk in his paths" (Isaiah 2:3), in order to "raise up unto myself a pure people, that will serve me in righteousness" (D&C 100:16). To do this, the covenant people have always been commanded to forsake the world and look to the Lord and His living prophet as the source of truth and guidance.

Central to this design is the requirement that Israel build a society that will maintain and promote the principles and power of righteousness to guarantee peace, prosperity, and safety and promote the fulness of the gospel. In short, whenever God gathers His people together, it is for the purpose of building Zion in their midst. Speaking on this subject, the Prophet Joseph Smith taught that "the building up of Zion is a cause that has interested the people of God in every age; it is a theme upon which prophets, priests and kings have dwelt with peculiar delight."[19]

According to the scriptures, Zion is "the city of the Lord" (Isaiah 60:14; D&C 97:19), the place of salvation (Isaiah 46:13), and the place of deliverance (Joel 2:32). It is a place of safety, and all who fight against her will be destroyed (1 Nephi 22:14; 2 Nephi 6:13, 27:3; D&C 45:68) because the Lord promises that "Zion shall not be moved out of her place" (D&C 101:17). Zion holds the promises of the Lord to His people (D&C 57:2) and is a place where "beauty and holiness" flourish (D&C 82:14; 64:41). Zion rests in the New Jerusalem (D&C 84:2), from which the Lord will give His law (Isaiah 2:3; 2 Nephi 14:3). Zion cannot be established on worldly philosophies and schemes but operates by the "principles of the law of the celestial kingdom" (D&C 105:5). Her citizens are characterized as "the pure in heart" (D&C 97:21) who are of "one heart and one mind, and [dwell] in righteousness," with "no poor among them" (Moses 7:18). Because of this the Lord bestows great glory upon her (D&C 133:32, 136:31).

In short, Zion is a group of people who have covenanted with the Lord to do His will and live after the celestial order of life. When they do this, He blesses them with the same endowment given to Enoch and his city and establishes a full ministrative system among them so that they are able, through His "providence," to "stand independent above all other creatures beneath the celestial world" (D&C 78:14).

The scriptures also teach that Zion has an opposite, an antithesis, designated by the term Babylon. Babylon signifies the wickedness of the world in all its forms and expressions. For example, the Lord refers to Babylon as "the apostate, the whore" and reveals that "the enemy, even Satan, sitteth to reign" there (D&C 86:3). John the Revelator states that Babylon is the "mother of harlots and abominations of the earth" (Revelation 17:5). Jacob relied on Isaiah to show that the destruction of Babylon in the last days will be "as when God overthrew Sodom and Gomorrah" (2 Nephi 23:19). In the preface to the Doctrine and Covenants, the Lord condemns the world because its inhabitants "seek not the Lord to establish his righteousness, but every man walketh in his own way, and after the image of his own god, whose image is in the likeness of the world, and whose substance is that of an idol, which waxeth old and shall perish in Babylon, even Babylon the great, which shall fall" (D&C 1:16).

Babylon includes the pursuit of earthly riches and power as opposed to, or in indifference to, God. It includes the sexual perversions of the world, such as pornography, infidelity, fornication, homosexuality, as well as more subtle impurities. Aspiring to the prestige and honors of men likewise belongs to Babylon—for example, neglecting family and Church service for career, or concerning oneself more with what others think than what God thinks. Babylon focuses on the outward appearance rather than the substance of the soul and is often characterized by the gaudy and vulgar fashions, style, glamour, art, and music of the world.

It is no surprise, then, that Babylon aspires to the flatterings, vanity, conquest, prestige, and honors of the world. Nothing is more important than this pursuit to those caught up in Babylon. The peace of the Spirit, the happiness of the gospel, and the love of God and one's fellow beings never seems enough to satisfy those who are so easily seduced by the trappings and enticements of the world. They believe that pleasure and success only come by external recognition, and Babylon promises this validation, acceptance, security, and belonging. Of course, the price demanded for this security is one's soul, but many are willing to pay.

All that Babylon is can be summed up in one word: pride. As President Ezra Taft Benson declared, the essence of pride is enmity (or hatred) "toward God and enmity toward our fellowmen. Those who embrace Babylon selfishly pit their own desires and wills against God. . . . The proud stand more in fear of men's judgment than of God's judgment. . . .

'What will men think of me?' weighs heavier than 'What will God think of me?'" For example, the proud in Babylon "cannot accept the authority of God giving direction to their lives. . . . They pit their perceptions of truth against God's great knowledge, their abilities versus God's priesthood power, their accomplishments against His mighty works."[20]

Ironically, becoming so engrossed in seeking the honors and validation of men requires a person to simultaneously disregard the very people he hopes to impress. To stand out in Babylon, we must *step on* others. Babylon is so rooted in the notion of scarcity and cutthroat competition—for riches, for power, for prestige, for attention—that in order to succeed, others must fail.

President Benson insightfully identified this attitude when he wrote, "The proud make every man their adversary by pitting their intellects, opinions, works, wealth, talents, or any other worldly measuring device against others. In the words of C. S. Lewis: 'Pride gets no pleasure out of having something, only out of having more of it than the next man. . . . It is the comparison that makes you proud: the pleasure of being above the rest. Once the element of competition has gone, pride has gone.'" Concluding his masterful discourse on pride, President Benson declared, "My dear brethren and sisters, we must prepare to redeem Zion. It was essentially the sin of pride that kept us from establishing Zion in the days of the Prophet Joseph Smith. . . . *Pride is the great stumbling block to Zion.* I repeat: *Pride is the great stumbling block to Zion.*"[21]

Zion and Babylon stand diametrically opposed to one another. Where one is, the other cannot be. Therefore, we must reject the worldliness of Babylon and cleave unto Zion. And although Zion as a completely operational society has not yet been fully established in this dispensation, the call to forsake the wickedness of the world so that we, as the Lord's covenant people, may build Zion remains extended to us. The Lord commands His Saints, "Go ye out from Babylon. Be ye clean that bear the vessels of the Lord. . . . Go ye out from among the nations, even from Babylon, from the midst of wickedness, which is spiritual Babylon" (D&C 133:5, 14).

Israel's command to leave Babylon and flee to Zion does not necessarily involve a physical departure. For example, when the Lord commanded Moses to take Israel out of Egypt, he was to lead them geographically from the banks of the Nile and, more important, to lead their hearts away from the corrupt teachings, traditions, and practices of Egypt. Similarly, although we have not been directed to leave our homes and vocations and gather in remote, secluded locations far removed from mainstream society, we are to remove ourselves from the wicked culture, corrupt philosophies, and false traditions of the world in which we now live.

For many, if not nearly all, this is a daunting task. Our modern society has become so accustomed to the ways of the world, so steeped in its mind-set, and so raised on its attitudes and practices that some Latter-day Saints have come to believe that the Lord intends us now to embrace the world and all its glory, relying on the gospel merely to provide general moral guidance and basic spiritual fulfillment. Nothing could be further from the truth. President Hinckley declared that we "have moved too far toward the mainstream of society."[22]

President James E. Faust likewise expressed that in our society "many sacred values have been eroded. . . . The mainstream of society has become more tolerant, even accepting, of conduct that Jesus, Moses, the Prophet Joseph Smith, and other prophets have warned against since the beginning of human history. We should not allow our personal values to erode, even if others think we are peculiar. We have always been regarded as a peculiar people. However, being spiritually correct is much better than being politically correct. Of course, as individuals and as a people we want to be liked and respected. But we cannot be in the mainstream of society if it means abandoning those righteous principles which thundered down from Sinai, later to be refined by the Savior, and subsequently taught by modern prophets. We should only fear offending God and His Son, Jesus Christ, who is the head of this Church."[23]

The Lord warned, "All the proud and they that do wickedly shall be as stubble; and I will burn them up, for I am the Lord of Hosts; and I will not spare any that remain in Babylon" (D&C 64:24).

Thankfully, escaping this judgment is simple. Applying the teachings of the Book of Mormon, President Benson taught that we must "cleanse the inner vessel by conquering pride (Alma 6:2–4) [and] yield 'to the enticings of the Holy Spirit,' put off the prideful 'natural man,' become 'a saint through the atonement of Christ the Lord,' and become 'as a child, submissive, meek, humble' (Mosiah 3:19)."[24]

Doubly Minded

One great challenge most of us struggle with is conflicting allegiance. While we love the Lord and strive to live the gospel, we also love the things of the world and refuse to give them up. This inner conflict keeps us from truly knowing Christ and enjoying the full benefits of the Holy Ghost in our lives. It keeps us from building Zion. In his epistle, John commanded, "Love not the world, neither the things that are in the world. If any man love the world, the love of the Father is not in him" (1 John 2:15).

"No man can serve two masters," Jesus taught (Matthew 6:24) because, as James explained, "a double minded man is unstable in all his ways" (James 1:8). We must each decide to follow one side and forsake the other; if we seek eternal life, we must choose the Lord and forsake the world. Although as a rule this does not occur overnight, we tend too easily to convince ourselves that we are committed to the Lord and His Church while in some cases choosing the things of the world. An astute observer of LDS culture once commented that many of us "want to live in Zion but keep a winter home in Babylon."[25]

The conflict between choosing the Lord and choosing the world applies poignantly to sustaining the living prophet. Some members, for example, choose to believe and follow portions of what the prophet teaches but dismiss those things that the world tells them are without real merit. And although this "selective obedience" may work for a while, it eventually leads to downfall. It lulls people "into carnal security" (2 Nephi 28:21), leading them to believe that they are right with the Lord and His Church until they reach a crisis moment when they find they cannot sustain the prophet in all things. They discover that they have failed to develop sufficient faith in the Lord's living oracle because they have refused to "lay aside the things of this world, and seek for the things of a better" (D&C 25:10).

Worldly Wisdom vs. the Living Prophet

Chapter 4 established that the living prophet can speak about any subject, regardless of his personal expertise in that particular area. He does this because the wisdom is never his alone, but the Lord's, and we are bound by covenant to believe and obey. But what if the living prophet, speaking by the keys of his calling, teaches something that conflicts with the learning, opinions, or expertise of the world? What if he teaches something that conflicts with our own personal opinions or preferences? To these pointed questions, only one sure response keeps us in good standing with the Lord and in tune with His Holy Spirit: "The living prophet is right."

To the world at large, and even to some members of the Church, this approach seems naive and foolish, but the Lord has always required His people to sustain the prophet, even when his teachings and counsel seem ridiculous to the world. After all, the Lord declared that the gospel would "be proclaimed by the weak and the simple unto the ends of the world, and before kings and rulers" (D&C 1:23). The history of mankind, in fact, seems to be defined by assumptions that the servants of God erred because they taught that which conflicted with traditional worldly wisdom.

For example, all the inhabitants of the earth save eight people believed Noah was foolish for building the ark. They refused to accept the notion that the planet's human population, along with its nonmarine animal life, could be destroyed by a flood. Egypt, the most advanced and hailed nation on earth at the time, scoffed at Moses when he warned of plagues and judgments that would follow if Pharaoh did not release Israel. The Sadducees considered the resurrection nothing more than a fairy tale when Christ preached the doctrine, and the wicked and stubborn among the Nephites never expected a night to become day at the birth of the Savior. Experts in the Prophet Joseph Smith's day considered the Word of Wisdom foolish because it conflicted with established scientific thinking, as did his anthropological claims about the ancient Nephites in the Americas.

These few examples of worldly wisdom conflicting with the words of the prophets share a common denominator: they all came to naught, while the words of the prophets were proven in the end. But how do these examples compare to our day with its progressive thinking, modern scientific theories, and advanced technology? We only need compare the doctrines of the Church and the teachings of the living prophet with the current ideas and approaches of the world to see that the kingdom is far removed from the world, and Babylon is still Babylon.

An alarming problem occurs when Church members choose to embrace the philosophies and learning of the world in opposition to the living prophet. At best, these misguided souls attempt to justify and reconcile their religion with their learning instead of measuring their worldly knowledge by the standard set by the living prophet. At worst, they altogether reject those teachings and counsels of the prophet that run counter to the standard accepted wisdom of the world; they consider the prophet's words foolish and place their trust in the arm of the flesh.

Jacob, the brother of Nephi, aptly described the wisdom of Babylon and decried its influence in the latter days when he wrote, "O that cunning plan of the evil one! O the vainness, and the frailties, and the foolishness of men! When they are learned they think they are wise, and they hearken not unto the counsel of God, for they set it aside, supposing they know of themselves, wherefore, their wisdom is foolishness and it profiteth them not. And they shall perish. But" he added, *"to be learned is good if they hearken unto the counsels of God"* (2 Nephi 9:28–29; emphasis added).

Indeed, learning and knowledge are good, including the opportunities available in the world for education and training. President Gordon B. Hinckley admonished, "It is so important that you young men and you young women get all of the education that you can. . . . Education is the key which will unlock the door of opportunity for you. . . . Take advantage of every educational opportunity that you can possibly afford, and you fathers and mothers, encourage your sons and daughters to gain an education which will bless their lives."[26]

But the danger with worldly education lies in the contamination of true principles with error and even wickedness. For example, during my first semester of college, before I transferred to BYU, I took a class from an exceptionally gifted professor who had been trained at some of the finest institutions in the world. I learned much from him and from his classes. In his political philosophy class we discussed the concept of separation of church and state. He propagated the notion that the federal government should be independent of the control or inappropriate influence of churches or religion. This, of course, reflects the thinking of the Founding Fathers of the United States.

However, he pushed this idea further and taught that religion should play no role in government and that to adopt religious principles into politics is to destroy objective and stable government. He continued, arguing that religion was merely a crutch for troubled or lonely people and that the truly enlightened individual relies on his own abilities and fortitude to thrive and survive. This, of course, is nonsense.[27] But it greatly affected several impressionable young minds in the class. Gratefully, I had the gospel of Christ to discern between truth and error, but others did not. Although this professor would never have purposely misled his students, he did much damage by mixing truth with the false teachings and philosophies of the world.

Another example may be more poignant. Much controversy has arisen recently over the issue of homosexuality and same-sex marriage. Current worldly thinking supports homosexuality and the right to same-sex marriage based on the belief that the expression and practice of homosexuality is a right, devoid of any moral choice or implication. Many scholars, physicians, politicians, and lawyers argue that the homosexual community has every right to practice, promote, and legalize its lifestyle, arguing that to deny people the right to live as they choose is morally reprehensible.

In contrast to this position, the Church has officially stated the Lord's word on the subject. For example, President Faust explained, "There is some widely accepted theory extant that homosexuality is inherited. How can this be? No scientific evidence demonstrates absolutely that this is so. Besides, if it were so, it would frustrate the whole plan of mortal happiness. Our designation as men or women began before this world was. In contrast to the socially accepted doctrine that homosexuality is inborn, a number of respectable authorities contend that homosexuality is not acquired by birth. The false belief of inborn homosexual orientation denies to repentant souls the opportunity to change and will ultimately lead to discouragement, disappointment, and despair."[28]

He went on to state that "any alternatives to the legal and loving marriage between a man and a woman are helping to unravel the fabric of human society. I am sure this is pleasing to the devil. The fabric I refer to is the family. These so-called alternative lifestyles must not be accepted as right, because they frustrate God's commandment for a life-giving union of male and female within a legal marriage as stated in Genesis. If practiced by all adults, these lifestyles would mean the end of the human family."[29]

In answer to the question, "What is your Church's attitude toward homosexuality?" President Hinckley declared:

> In the first place, we believe that marriage between a man and a woman is ordained of God. . . . People inquire about our position on those who consider themselves so-called gays and lesbians. My response is that we love them as sons and daughters of God. . . . We want to help these people, to strengthen them, to assist them with their problems and to help them with their difficulties. But we cannot stand idle if they indulge in immoral activity, if they try to uphold and defend and live in a so-called same-sex marriage situation. To permit such would be to make light of the very serious and sacred foundation of God-sanctioned marriage and its very purpose, the rearing of families.[30]

Both of these statements are clear and unequivocal. There is simply no way to reconcile the revealed teachings of the living prophet with the current thinking of the world on the issue of homosexuality and same-sex marriage. One is right and one is wrong. We must decide whether God has a prophet to whom He reveals His truth and His will. And if we believe He does, we must decide whether that prophet stands at the head of this Church and kingdom. If we have a testimony of this, the debate is over. Our personal opinions, preferences, desires, attitudes, logic, and learning take a backseat to the will of the Lord revealed through His prophet.

And yet, many continue to struggle with this because of their deep-seated reliance on the wisdom of the world. They have placed such confidence in what they have learned that they feel caught off guard or threatened by teachings that force them to change, rethink, and relearn what they have spent years believing—in short, to stretch outside their comfort zones. However, they must finally accept the truth that "the wisdom of this world is foolishness with God. For it is written, He taketh the wise in their own craftiness. And again, The Lord knoweth the thoughts of the wise, that they are vain. Therefore let no man glory in men" (1 Corinthians 3:19–21).

Instead of struggling to remain in our individual comfort zones, we must awaken to the reality that the only sure comfort comes from knowing that God loves us enough to give us a living prophet to lead us and reveal truth to us. And while we can learn great things by studying the knowledge of the world, we must first have a firm grounding in the truths of the gospel and judge everything we learn and experience by that standard.

Explaining the appropriate relationship between the gospel and the learning of the world, President Joseph F. Smith explained: "Our . . . people are diligent students. They reach out after truth and knowledge with commendable zeal, and in so doing they must necessarily adopt for temporary use, many theories of men. As long, however, as they recognize them as scaffolding useful for research purposes, there can be no special harm in them. It is when these theories are settled upon as basic truth that trouble appears, and the searcher then stands in grave danger of being led hopelessly from the right way."[31]

Continuing, President Smith declared: "The Church holds to the definite authority of divine revelation which must be the standard; and that, so-called 'Science' has changed from age to age in its deductions, and as divine revelation is truth, and must abide forever, views as to the lesser should conform to the positive statements of the greater, and, further, that in institutions founded by the Church for the teaching of theology, as well as other branches of education, its instructors must be in harmony in their teachings with its principles and doctrines."[32]

The Standard of Truth

The best way to stay in tune with the Lord is to keep the living prophet as our standard of truth. Webster's defines a standard as (1) "an ensign" and (2) "something set up and established by authority as a rule for the measure of quantity, value, or quality." These definitions appropriately characterize the office of the living prophet.

First, an ensign is a visible object lifted up, around which people rally. The prophet is the one person on earth around whom the world's inhabitants are commanded to rally. Indeed, we are to look to him as the one lifted up by the Lord to gather us, lead us, and direct us. Second, the prophet—more specifically his counsel and teachings—stands as the measuring rod by which truth, doctrine, commandment, practice, and behavior must be evaluated. According to President Faust, the Holy Ghost and "the guidance of modern prophets, provide true standards of conduct."[33]

If we look to the living prophet—not to be "commanded in all things" but to discover appropriate actions and limitations—we will stay in harmony with the Lord and His Holy Spirit. Regardless of our friends, neighbors, family, traditions, customs, preferences, learning, training, opinions, or the world at large, the living prophet sets the standard—indeed, *is* the standard under Christ—by which we must measure truth.

President Hinckley illustrated this very principle using "The Family: A Proclamation to the World" as an example. He stated:

> With so much of sophistry that is passed off as truth, with so much of deception concerning standards and values, with so much of allurement and enticement to take on the slow stain of the world, we have felt to warn and forewarn. In furtherance of this we of the First Presidency and the Council of the Twelve Apostles now issue a proclamation to the Church and to the world as a declaration and reaffirmation of standards, doctrines, and practices relative to the family which the prophets, seers, and revelators of this church have repeatedly stated throughout its history.[34]

President George Albert Smith aptly summed up our responsibility to keep the living prophets as our standard of truth. He stated, "There is only one pathway of safety for me in this day and that is to follow those whom the Lord has appointed to lead. I may have my own ideas and opinions, I may set up my own judgment with reference to things, but I know that when my judgment conflicts with the teachings of those that the Lord has given to us to point the way, I should change my course. If I desire salvation, I will follow the leaders that our Heavenly Father has given to us."[35]

Steer Clear of Apostasy

As discussed in chapter 9, apostasy is perhaps the most damaging way we reject the living prophet and remove ourselves from the Lord. To find fault with the living prophet and other priesthood leaders is to find fault with the Lord. By the same token, rejecting the living prophet and other priesthood leaders is to reject the Lord. The Lord said of those who reject him, "I will also reject [you]" (Hosea 4:6).

The best and surest way to steer clear of apostasy is to follow the prophet's lead in all things. He sets the bounds and limits of what is appropriate doctrine and practice in the Church. And regardless of what others may consider appropriate or expedient, the Lord only recognizes and sustains actions sanctioned by the living prophet.

Apostasy never begins with outright rejection of our leaders. Instead, we start down the road to apostasy when we begin to murmur in our own mind. The way to avoid this is to first commit to sustaining the living prophet and other leaders, even if this means suppressing the desire to oppose them. Second, when we get the slightest inclination to doubt or murmur against priesthood leaders, we must consciously decide to let it go. If we allow ourselves to begin to contemplate the possibility that we are right while our leaders are out of harmony, we take the first step away from the Lord and the security of His Spirit.

In connection with preventing apostasy in thought, we must avoid situations and people who encourage apostasy. The danger lies where others can influence us to consider our leaders in a negative light. This influence may even come from those we care for and respect. But we must not allow anything or anyone to deter us from our commitment to sustain the living prophet.

A family I knew fell into this trap. The husband embarked down the road to apostasy because he claimed to have a special knowledge that the current living prophet was no longer leading the Church. Although his wife and children were faithful and refused to believe what he claimed, he eventually managed to talk them into leaving the Church. After years of disappointment and heartache, the wife admitted that she never intended to leave the Church, nor allow her husband's apostasy to influence her children. She also expressed the desire to regain her membership but despaired that her husband would never allow it. She had esteemed her husband above the living prophet and had chosen to sustain him in his apostasy rather than the Lord's prophet in righteousness.

I became acquainted with an intelligent young man with great spiritual capacity and deep scriptural knowledge. He began affiliating with a group of citizens who held similar political beliefs that he did. After meeting a few of them, I expressed concern over their more overtly apostate positions. My friend assured me that he was fully aware that some of their ideas were, as he put it, "on the fringe," but he justified his association by explaining that much of what they espoused was in harmony with the gospel. As he spent more time with his new cadre, he spent more time criticizing the Church, its leadership, and just about everything associated with it. Sadly, I recently discovered that he had left the Church and rejected the divine calling of the living prophet.

Each of us has to decide which situations are unacceptable and incompatible with our commitment to the living prophet and other Church leaders, but we must take great care to discern if and when to finally avoid them and then be prepared to do so. In the end, our duty to the living prophet must always supersede our allegiance to others because the Lord acknowledges and sustains His appointed representative above all others on earth.

This does not mean that we should simply forsake those who struggle with their faith or who do not believe as we do. In fact, our example, love, and support can do much to strengthen those who falter and may help to convert the nonbeliever. However, longsuffering has its limits. And if a situation requires allegiance to one side or the other, we need to have the conviction to follow the Lord and His representative.

Stay Up-to-Date with the Living Prophet

One of the great liabilities of human nature is the propensity to take wonderful things for granted. Having a living prophet is no exception. We live in a time long dreamed of and prayed for by the honest in heart in ages past. The gospel has been restored to the earth, and prophets and apostles walk the earth today speaking in the authority of the God of heaven.

And yet, many are complacent about this great gift. They forget how long humanity sat deprived of priesthood authority and the saving ordinances of the gospel. They fail to fully appreciate that God speaks through a living prophet, whose voice we can hear and whose words we can read and study—something that millions could not for many centuries. Think of it: We have access to living truth, restored and revealed in the dispensation of the fulness of times.

How then do we show gratitude for this marvelous blessing and avoid taking it for granted? We must study the words and teachings of the prophet. One way to do this is by studying the scriptures—the writings of the ancient prophets and of our modern-day Church prophets in the Doctrine and Covenants. In addition, we must study the teachings of Church presidents and other inspired leaders who speak under their direction.

The best way to keep up to date with the living prophet is to listen to him speak. President Young showed the importance of this endeavor when he wrote, "In my experience I never let an opportunity pass of getting with the Prophet Joseph and hearing him speak in public or in private, so that I might draw understanding from the fountain from which he spoke, that I might have it and bring it forth when it was needed. . . . Such moments were more precious to me than all the wealth of the world. . . . This is the secret of success of your humble servant."[36]

The best place to listen to the living prophet, of course, is at general conference. In fact, listening to or reading general conference addresses is not just a privilege; rather, it is a responsibility. It is the time and place that each member of the Church can receive living truth and revelation in order to know what the Lord has to give through the living prophet.

President Spencer W. Kimball explained the importance of general conference when he counseled, "Now as we conclude this general conference, let us all give heed to what was said to us. Let us assume the counsel given applies to us, to me. Let us hearken to those we sustain as prophets and seers, as well as the other brethren, as if our eternal life depended upon it, because it does! . . . May I stress again the value of reading the addresses given at our general conferences in the *Ensign* magazine."[37]

President Benson admonished, "For the next six months, your conference edition of the *Ensign* should stand next to your standard works and be referred to frequently. As . . . Harold B. Lee said, we should let these conference addresses 'be [our] guide . . . during these next six months.' These are the important matters the Lord sees fit to reveal to this people this day."[38]

In addition to conference, many other opportunities exist to hear the prophet's words. Firesides, broadcasts, special publications, and declarations provide chances to learn from our prophet firsthand and remain current with what he would have us know.

But simply showing up to hear what the Lord's oracle has to say is only the first step. We also have a responsibility to prepare ourselves by the Spirit beforehand in order to receive all that the Lord wishes us to know. For example, the Prophet Joseph Smith instructed those who planned to attend the dedication of the Kirtland Temple to prepare themselves spiritually so they could receive and understand the great manifestations of power and glory that were to be poured out during that dedication. Before giving the Prophet a crucial commandment, the Lord told him to "prepare thy heart to receive and obey the instructions which I am about to give unto you" (D&C 132:3).

We can also take an example from the Book of Mormon. After the resurrected Savior appeared to the Nephites and taught them the Sermon on the Mount, He commanded them to "go ye unto your homes, and ponder the things which I have said, and ask of the Father, in my name, that ye may understand, and *prepare your minds for the morrow,* and I come unto you again" (3 Nephi 17:3; emphasis added). Fasting, reading what the prophet has previously taught, praying to understand what will yet be taught and to gain a witness of it are ways to prepare to listen and receive the words of the prophet.

Doing this allows us not only to receive what is spoken by the prophet, but it also allows the Lord to open more to us through insight and revelation based on the prophet's words. Though we may hear the same talk or counsel, the Spirit can help each of us understand and apply those words in ways specific to our personal needs and according to our levels of faith, knowledge, and preparedness.

Learning all that the Lord's prophets have taught is not just a right, it is a responsibility. The Prophet Joseph Smith taught that when "God offers a blessing or knowledge to a man, and he refuses to receive it, he will be damned."[39] To illustrate this point, the Prophet used ancient Israel as a model. Although Moses led them from slavery, he had little success liberating them from the mind-set and attitudes to which they had grown accustomed in Egypt. They were so used to being told what to do and how to do it under their Egyptian masters that they forgot how to take personal responsibility, initiative, and interest in their personal salvation.

When offered the sacred blessing of liberty and a personal stake in their earthly governance and eternal destiny, most of them refused, preferring the same arrangement as in Egypt—only under a different taskmaster. Even when the great Jehovah offered to speak to His people personally and give them the law of Zion and the fulness of the priesthood, "the Israelites prayed that God would speak to Moses and not to them." They preferred to remain content, with full bellies, the basic comforts of the world, and their narrow perceptions of reality, than to know the living God, discover eternal truths, and sacrifice all things necessary to becoming a Zion people and being endowed with glory from on high. In consequence of this stubbornness and lack of interest in personal salvation, Joseph revealed that the Lord "cursed them with a carnal law."[40]

The Prophet Joseph referenced the account of the children of Israel for a reason. He was trying to show that a similarity exists between them and us. We are of the same lineage; indeed, they are our ancestors. And as such, we share most of their strengths and weaknesses. We too tend to leave our personal salvation to others. We sometimes avoid the real responsibility of seeking truth and light for ourselves when we would rather be told what we absolutely must do and what we absolutely must believe in order to qualify for exaltation.

Do we really seek for ourselves to know what the living prophet has taught on various issues and subjects? Do we search into the truths his predecessors have revealed? Just because a particular subject was not included in a recent conference address does not diminish the value or weight of a truth revealed through God's authorized mouthpiece at an earlier time.

Some consider it a chore to learn all that the prophets have revealed, but it is a great blessing and a fascinating adventure. And though it requires faith, sacrifice, work, and commitment, the rewards we receive are greater than we can now understand. I think fondly on a time in my life when I began to acquire a greater hunger for the mysteries of God. I listened to conference and searched the scriptures voraciously. But when I took the time to sift through the writings, talks, and teachings of past Church presidents—especially the Prophet Joseph Smith—I developed a deeper perspective of the gospel and understood Christ and the plan of happiness in ways I never had before. That isn't to say that the living prophet's words could not give us the same perspective and depth; the Lord simply blessed me with more profound insight than I had at that point through truths formerly revealed by past prophets.

Discovering for ourselves what the prophets have revealed is so important that while teaching about the essential character of agency and personal responsibility, the Prophet Joseph Smith declared:

> Search the revelations of God; study the prophecies, and rejoice that God grants unto the world Seers and prophets. They are they who saw the mysteries of godliness; . . . and they saw the heaven and the earth flee away to make room for the city of God, when the righteous received an inheritance in eternity. And, fellow sojourners upon earth, it is your privilege to purify yourselves and come up to the same glory, and see for yourselves, and know for yourselves. Ask and it shall be given you; seek and ye shall find; knock, and it shall be opened unto you.[41]

Accept the Prophet's Invitation to Come Back if You Have Fallen Away

Activity in the Church remains an obvious prerequisite to sustaining the prophet. But many struggle with activity or challenges to their membership. Some have left the Church after making poor choices in life, others have dropped out because they have allowed themselves to become offended with someone in the Church, while still others have been forced out by excommunication or similar disciplinary action.

Notwithstanding the distance you may feel from the Lord and His Church, He wants us all to return to Him and enjoy the full blessings the gospel offers. It is never too late for anyone who desires to return. Even if you can only consider the possibility of returning, full repentance and fellowship is well within your grasp. The Savior and His priesthood representatives on earth desire to bring those who have fallen away back into activity and fellowship. And they stand with open arms ready to do so.

Comparing those who have strayed from the Church to lost sheep, the Savior taught, "What man of you, having an hundred sheep, if he lose one of them, doth not leave the ninety and nine in the wilderness, and go after that which is lost, until he find it? And when he hath found it, he layeth it on his shoulders, rejoicing. And when he cometh home, he calleth together his friends and neighbours, saying unto them, Rejoice with me: for I have found my sheep which was lost." Then, to make the point, the Master concluded, "I say unto you, that likewise joy shall be in heaven over one sinner that repenteth, more than over ninety and nine just persons, which need no repentance" (Luke 15:4–7).

Speaking in general conference, President Faust implored:

> If there are any of you who do not enjoy fellowship with us in the gospel of Jesus Christ, we invite you to seek to know what instilled such great faith in your ancestors and what motivated them to willingly pay such a terrible price for their membership in this Church. To those who have been offended or lost interest or who have turned away for any reason, we invite all of you to join in full fellowship again with us. The faithful members, with all their faults and failings, are humbly striving to do God's holy work across the world. We need your help in the great struggle against the powers of darkness so prevalent in the world today. In becoming a part of this work, you can all satisfy the deepest yearnings of your souls. You can come to know the personal comfort that can be found in seeking the sacred and holy things of God. You can enjoy the blessings and covenants administered in the holy temples. You can have great meaning and purpose in your lives, even in the profane world in which we live. You can have strength of character so that you can act for yourselves and not be acted upon.[42]

The first step for you who desire to return to the fold is to go to Church. Seek out your bishop and discuss with him the further necessary steps to reestablishing your full membership and activity in the kingdom. He is the person empowered to represent the living prophet, and ultimately the Savior, on your behalf. Humbly listen and heed his direction. This will give you power to return and remain and enjoy the choice blessings of fellowship with the Saints of God.

Even if you have not actually left the Church but have struggled in some way—with teachings, standards, or other priesthood leaders—let go of the past and recommit now. Accept the invitation to come back by returning in your heart and mind to full fellowship. Allow yourself to sustain the living prophet in all things, and make him the standard of truth in your life.

Notes

1. N. Eldon Tanner, "The Debate Is Over," *Ensign,* August 1979, 2.
2. Robert D. Hales, "Hear the Prophet's Voice and Obey," *Ensign,* May 1995, 15.
3. David O. McKay, in Conference Reports of The Church of Jesus Christ of

Latter-day Saints (Salt Lake City: The Church of Jesus Christ of Latter-day Saints, 1898 to present), October 1914, 87–88.

4. Rex Pinegar, "The Simple Things," *Ensign,* November 1994, 80.
5. Brigham Young, in *Journal of Discourses,* 26 vols. (London: Latter-day Saints' Book Depot, 1854–86), 9:150.
6. Joseph Smith, *Teachings of the Prophet Joseph Smith,* sel. Joseph Fielding Smith (Salt Lake City: Deseret Book, 1976), 253.
7. Ibid., 322; emphasis added.
8. Neal A. Maxwell, "Settle This in Your Hearts," *Ensign,* November 1992, 65.
9. Joseph F. Smith, in *Journal of Discourses,* 25:245.
10. Neal A. Maxwell, "Swallowed Up in the Will of the Father," *Ensign,* November 1995, 22.
11. Joshua Reuben Clark, *Diaries and Records of Joshua R. Clark and Mary Louisa Woolley Clark* (Provo, Utah: Brigham Young University, 1939–40), 1.
12. Smith, *Teachings,* 256.
13. Ibid., 27.
14. Ibid., 332.
15. Ibid., 187–88.
16. Brigham Young, in *Journal of Discourses,* 9:289.
17. Wilford Woodruff, *The Discourses of Wilford Woodruff,* ed. G. Homer Duram (Salt Lake City: Bookcraft, 1969), 212–23.
18. Brigham Young, in *Journal of Discourses,* 9:289.
19. Smith, *Teachings,* 231.
20. Ezra Taft Benson, "Beware of Pride," *Ensign,* May 1989, 4–5.
21. Ibid., 4, 7; emphasis added.
22. Gordon B. Hinckley, "Look to the Future," *Ensign,* November 1997, 69.
23. James E. Faust, "Search Me, O God, and Know My Heart," *Ensign,* May 1998, 17.
24. Benson, "Beware of Pride," 4.
25. Ardeth Kapp, at a missionary fireside in Victoria, British Columbia, Canada, 1994.
26. Gordon B. Hinckley, "Inspirational Thoughts," *Ensign,* June 1999, 2.
27. For example, President Benson proclaimed the following as the living prophet: "The Book of Mormon warns us relative to our living in this free land: 'Wherefore, this land is consecrated unto him whom he shall bring. And if it so be that they shall serve him according to the commandments which he hath given, it shall be a land of liberty unto them; wherefore, they shall never be brought down into captivity; if so, it shall be because of iniquity; for if iniquity shall abound cursed shall be the land for their sakes, but unto the righteous it shall be blessed forever' (2 Nephi 1:7). 'And now,' warned Moroni, 'we can behold the decrees of God concerning this land, that it is a land of promise; and whatsoever nation shall possess it shall serve God, or they shall be swept off when the fulness of his wrath shall come upon them. And the fulness of his wrath cometh upon them when they are ripened in iniquity' (Ether 2:9)" ("Our Divine Constitution," *Ensign,* November 1987, 4).

28. James E. Faust, "Serving the Lord and Resisting the Devil," *Ensign,* September 1995, 2.
29. Ibid.
30. Gordon B. Hinckley, "What Are People Asking about Us?" *Ensign,* November 1998, 70.
31. Joseph F. Smith, *Gospel Doctrine: Selections from the Sermons and Writings of Joseph F. Smith* (Salt Lake City: Deseret Book, 1971), 38.
32. Ibid.
33. James E. Faust, "The Gift of the Holy Ghost—A Sure Compass," *Ensign,* May 1989, 31.
34. Gordon B. Hinckley, "Stand Strong against the Wiles of the World," *Ensign,* November 1995, 98.
35. George Albert Smith, in Conference Report, April 1937, 33.
36. Brigham Young, in *Journal of Discourses,* 12:269–70.
37. Spencer W. Kimball, "Listen to the Prophets," *Ensign,* May 1978, 77.
38. Ezra Taft Benson, "Come unto Christ, and Be Perfected in Him," *Ensign,* May 1988, 84.
39. Smith, *Teachings,* 322.
40. Ibid., 322.
41. Ibid., 12–13.
42. James E. Faust, "A Priceless Heritage," *Ensign,* July 2002, 2.

Conclusion

We stand at a crossroads—as a group of Saints, as a nation, as a brotherhood of mankind. The world grows darker and more dangerous, and the earth's inhabitants yearn for peace, truth, salvation, genuine leadership, stability, and lasting solutions to surmounting problems. We live in a time when men call good evil and evil good and are blown about by every wind of doctrine.

Yet there remains great hope—hope for lasting peace, hope for great joy, love, beauty, and prosperity. But this hope is to be found in Jesus Christ alone; no man-made institutions, programs, plans, or teachings can solve the ills of the world and guide us through perilous times. Only Christ and His kingdom, with its living power, light, and truth, offers a sure and steady course.

Central to the ministration of Christ's kingdom on earth is His living prophet. He is the one man raised up to lead the Saints of God and all the people of the world to safety and salvation. We need a living prophet more now than at any other time in the earth's history. And we can rejoice that we have one; we can thank God that our way is clear and sound as we follow and sustain the Lord's appointed shepherd.

It is neither weakness nor foolishness to rely on the guidance of the prophet and obey him in every thing he commands. None of us by our own strength has enough wisdom, knowledge, or power to stand alone in a world darkened by unbelief and the subtle snares of the adversary.

The Lord loves us and desires nothing but our happiness and the happiness of all mankind. If we heed Him by sustaining His prophet, He has promised His choicest blessings. They await us all. All that is left for us is to "choose you this day whom [we] will serve" (Joshua 24:15).

About the Author

Christopher Esseltine was born in St. Thomas, Ontario, Canada, and joined the Church when he was eighteen. After serving a mission in Arizona, he became deeply impressed by the founding fathers of the United States and the principles upon which the nation was founded. He moved to British Columbia before attending Brigham Young University, where he studied political science and history.

During his last semester, he met his wife, Adelia, whom he married three months later. That same semester, he was commissioned to write an American history textbook for high school and college students.

Chris worked in politics and education before attending Ave Maria School of Law in Ann Arbor, Michigan. There he focused his studies on the origins of American liberty and the political and legal ideas of Joseph Smith. He graduated in May 2005 and was later admitted to the Michigan Bar on the same day he realized his long-time dream of becoming a citizen of the United States.

Chris has written or edited several scholarly works and is currently preparing two works of fiction for publication. He has also lectured to several groups on political, historical, and religious topics.

He and his wife have a son, Joshua, and a daughter, Rachel.

0 26575 79522 6